AF514068

Tucholsky Wagner Zola Scott Sydow Fonatne Freud Schlegel Turgenev Wallace Twain Walther von der Vogelweide Fouqué Friedrich II. von Preußen Freiligrath Weber Frey Kant Ernst Fechner Fichte Weiße Rose von Fallersleben Frommel Richthofen Hölderlin Engels Fielding Eichendorff Tacitus Dumas Fehrs Faber Flaubert Eliasberg Ebner Eschenbach Feuerbach Maximilian I. von Habsburg Fock Eliot Zweig Ewald Vergil Goethe London Elisabeth von Österreich Mendelssohn Balzac Shakespeare Ganghofer Dostojewski Lichtenberg Rathenau Trackl Stevenson Doyle Gjellerup Tolstoi Hambruch Mommsen Lenz Thoma Hanrieder Droste-Hülshoff von Arnim Dach Verne Hägele Hauff Humboldt Reuter Karrillon Rousseau Hagen Hauptmann Garschin Gautier Defoe Baudelaire Damaschke Hebbel Descartes Hegel Kussmaul Herder Wolfram von Eschenbach Schopenhauer Dickens Darwin Rilke George Bronner Melville Grimm Jerome Bebel Campe Horváth Aristoteles Proust Voltaire Federer Bismarck Vigny Barlach Herodot Gengenbach Heine Storm Casanova Tersteegen Grillparzer Georgy Gilm Lessing Chamberlain Langbein Gryphius Brentano Lafontaine Strachwitz Claudius Schiller Kralik Iffland Sokrates Bellamy Schilling Katharina II. von Rußland Gerstäcker Raabe Gibbon Tschechow Löns Hesse Hoffmann Gogol Wilde Vulpius Gleim Luther Heym Hofmannsthal Morgenstern Klee Hölty Goedicke Roth Heyse Klopstock Kleist Luxemburg Puschkin Homer Mörike Musil La Roche Machiavelli Horaz Kierkegaard Kraft Navarra Aurel Kraus Musset Lamprecht Kind Moltke Kirchhoff Hugo Nestroy Marie de France Laotse Ipsen Liebknecht Nietzsche Nansen Ringelnatz Marx Lassalle Gorki Klett von Ossietzky Leibniz May vom Stein Lawrence Irving Petalozzi Platon Knigge Pückler Michelangelo Kafka Sachs Kock Poe Liebermann Korolenko de Sade Praetorius Mistral Zetkin

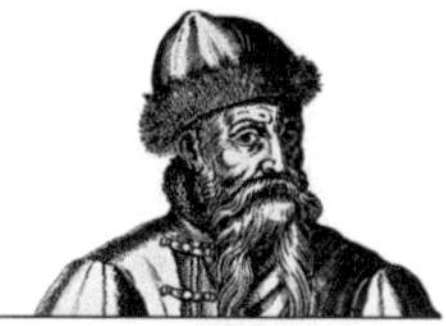

The publishing house tredition has created the series **TREDITION CLASSICS.** It contains classical literature works from over two thousand years. Most of these titles have been out of print and off the bookstore shelves for decades.

The book series is intended to preserve the cultural legacy and to promote the timeless works of classical literature. As a reader of a **TREDITION CLASSICS** book, the reader supports the mission to save many of the amazing works of world literature from oblivion.

The symbol of **TREDITION CLASSICS** is Johannes Gutenberg (1400 – 1468), the inventor of movable type printing.

With the series, tredition intends to make thousands of international literature classics available in printed format again – worldwide.

All books are available at book retailers worldwide in paperback and in hard-cover. For more information please visit: www.tredition.com

tredition was established in 2006 by Sandra Latusseck and Soenke Schulz. Based in Hamburg, Germany, tredition offers publishing solutions to authors and publishing houses, combined with worldwide distribution of printed and digital book content. tredition is uniquely positioned to enable authors and publishing houses to create books on their own terms and without conventional manufacturing risks.

For more information please visit: www.tredition.com

The Turkish Bath Its Design and Construction

Robert Owen Allsop

Imprint

This book is part of the TREDITION CLASSICS series.

Author: Robert Owen Allsop
Cover design: toepferschumann, Berlin (Germany)

Publisher: tredition GmbH, Hamburg (Germany)
ISBN: 978-3-8491-5004-4

www.tredition.com
www.tredition.de

Copyright:
The content of this book is sourced from the public domain.

The intention of the TREDITION CLASSICS series is to make world literature in the public domain available in printed format. Literary enthusiasts and organizations worldwide have scanned and digitally edited the original texts. tredition has subsequently formatted and redesigned the content into a modern reading layout. Therefore, we cannot guarantee the exact reproduction of the original format of a particular historic edition. Please also note that no modifications have been made to the spelling, therefore it may differ from the orthography used today.

PREFACE.

The present work originally appeared in the form of a series of illustrated articles in the columns of the *Building News*. It has been carefully revised and enlarged with the addition of much new matter. The object of the author in publishing the work in its present form is to provide, in addition to a text-book for the architect, a treatise which shall enable the public to form their own judgment as to the relative merits of the baths that compete for their patronage. The principles, herein enunciated, upon which good baths should be built, will be easily grasped by the ordinary reader; and the detailed plans and instructions will, it is hoped, supply such information as will enable the designer of baths to cope with the exigencies of any and every case with which he may be confronted.

37, Norfolk Street,
Strand, London.
March 1890.

CONTENTS.

CHAPTER I.

Introduction

CHAPTER II.

The General Requirements of a Public Bath

CHAPTER III.

The General Disposition of Plan of Public Baths

CHAPTER IV.

A Detailed Consideration of Features peculiar to the Bath

CHAPTER V.

Heating and Ventilation

CHAPTER VI.

Water-fittings and Appliances

CHAPTER VII.

Lighting, Decorating, and Furnishing

CHAPTER VIII.

The Turkish Bath in the House

CHAPTER IX.

The Bath in Public and Private Institutions, Etc.

CHAPTER X.

The Turkish Bath for Horses

LIST OF ILLUSTRATIONS.

FIG.

1. Turkish Baths, Savoy Hill, London
2. Turkish Baths, Charing Cross, London
3. Turkish Baths, Euston Road, London
4. A Plunge Bath
5. Methods of arranging Couches in Cooling Room
6. View of a small Furnace Chamber, with portion of wall broken away to show the "Convoluted" Stove
7. An Air Filter
8. Plans and Section of a Furnace Chamber, &c., for a Bath on the ordinary Hot-air Principle
9. Section of Hot Room, showing Foul-air Conduit
10. A Fireclay Heating Apparatus
11. Longitudinal Section of Sudatory Chambers
12. A Shampooing Basin
13. Valve for Regulating Temperature of Water
14. A Needle Bath
15. Spray, Wave, and Douche Baths
16. Regulating Valves for Needle, Douche, &c.
17. Bather's Shower Bath
18. Section and Plan of an Enamelled Iron Ceiling
19. Plans of Plunge Baths
20. Section of Benches in Hot Rooms, and in Cooling Room Divans
21. Furniture of a Turkish Bath
22. Plan of Mr. Urquhart's Small Private Bath and of the Hot Room at Sir Erasmus Wilson's Bath at Richmond Hill
23. Methods of constructing Turkish Baths in existing Houses
24. A complete Private Turkish Bath
25. Design for a Private Turkish Bath
26. Plan of the Baths at the Hotel Mont Dore, Bournemouth

27. Plan of the Great Northern Railway Company's Turkish Bath for Horses

[Pg 1]

THE TURKISH BATH.

CHAPTER I.

INTRODUCTION.

Since the revival of the bath of antiquity, and its introduction into this country under the name of the Turkish bath, this method of bathing has become very generally adopted; and although onward progress is rendered less rapid than it might be, by the wide-spread popular ignorance that ascribes an element of danger to the bath, erroneous impressions are being gradually removed, and the continual building of new baths testifies to the manner in which the institution flourishes on British soil.

To what extent the delusion concerning the supposed danger connected with this form of bathing is to be ascribed to popular ignorance and prejudice, or to the fact that baths of unsuitable design and construction, and of faulty heating and ventilation, are put before the public, it would be hard to say. Certain it is that the latter cause has done much—very much—injury.

I cannot but think that one of the chief obstacles to the progress of the bath in this country, is that little [Pg 2] or nothing has been written or said about its proper design, construction, and working, and that no full inquiry has been made into the best possible method of supplying heat to the bathers. As a consequence, we have had, and still have, placed before the public, and meeting with undeserved success, "Turkish baths" which are such only in name—unhealthy, ill-ventilated cellars, where the air, deteriorated at the outset by the heating apparatus, stagnates in the sudatory chambers, and becomes loaded with the exhalations and emanations of the bathers, and not unfrequently charged with a nauseating and disgusting odour. What wonder that we so often hear persons remark that they have tried the bath, but neither enjoyed it nor did it agree with them! The damaging effect of "baths" of this type on the prospects of the true bath is incalculable.

In the absence of enlightenment, however, thousands, convinced of the value and benefit of the bathing, periodically attend these miserable substitutes for properly-planned, hygienically-heated, and effectively-ventilated Turkish baths. Viewing any self-evident shortcomings as irremediable evils, ignorant of the true principles of bath construction, and knowing little or nothing of the physiological action of the bath, they have neither the means of ascertaining, nor the power to detect, the genuine article from the harmful substitute. With the public the best bath will be the most elaborate and most flashily decorated, and the moth-and-candle principle comes into play with striking semblance to the original type.

So much has been written and said about the arrange [Pg 3] ment, design, and working of the baths of the ancient Romans, and of the Oriental nations of to-day, that it will be superfluous and unnecessary here to enter upon the subject, fascinating though it be to any one interested in the building of modern baths. An intelligent study of old plans, and of the writings of those who have given their attention to the elucidation of the special purposes to which the various apartments of the Roman *Thermæ* were devoted, serves in no small degree to a complete understanding of the problems involved in the perfecting of the bath in modern times. So also with regard to the Hammam of the East, an acquaintance with its plan and working is equally instructive. But to fully elucidate the history of thermo-therapeutic architecture would require a volume of itself, since the many questions that present themselves to the student of ancient baths cannot be properly understood without considerable and lengthy description. Those desirous of studying the subject of the design of ancient and Oriental baths will find many works within easy reach. In his 'Manual of the Turkish Bath,' the late David Urquhart has given a most complete account of Eastern baths; and in Sir Erasmus Wilson's 'Eastern or Turkish Bath,' will be found a popular account of the sumptuous baths of antiquity, which will serve as an introduction to further researches with the aid of more abstruse works, such as Wollaston's 'Thermæ Romano-Britannicæ,' Cameron's 'Baths of the Romans,' and particularly the careful description of the Pompeian *Balneæ* in Sir William Gell's 'Pompeiana.' In the admirable works of Samuel Lysons, the Gloucestershire antiquary, will be [Pg 4] found interesting accounts of the remains of old Roman baths in this country; and in Daremberg and Saglio's 'Dictionnaire des Antiquités Grecques et Romaines,' is a most capable essay on ancient *Balneæ*. In Eastern travellers' books, desultory descriptions of the Oriental bath will be found; and in Owen Jones's work on the Palace of the Alhambra, at Granada, plans and sections are given of the elegant little bath that the Moorish builders erected therein.

For the purposes of this work, and for the sake of brevity and convenience, I have thought fit to adopt the following terms from the old Roman vocabulary, to designate the apartments of the modern bath. I respectively term the first, second, and third hot rooms, the *Tepidarium, Calidarium,* and *Laconicum.* Although the exact nature of the ancient Roman *laconicum* is still a question in debate, I have chosen to employ the term to designate herein the hottest of the hot. The washing room I call the *Lavatorium*; the cooling room, the *Frigidarium*; and the separate dressing room, the *Apodyterium.*

The modern "Turkish bath" is rather a revival of the Roman bath, than that of the East. Among the Orientals, the air of the sudorific chambers is charged more or less heavily with vapour. In the ancient Roman bath, the atmosphere must have been more or less dry. And it has been decided by physiologists and physicians of the hydropathic school, that the air of the bath cannot be too free of all moisture. With a perfectly dry atmosphere a high degree of heat can be borne, and the dryness moreover is conducive to perspiration. This [Pg 5] absolute need for a dry atmosphere in the bath will be found fully explained in an admirable work by Dr. W.B. Hunter, M.D., entitled 'The Turkish Bath: its Uses and Abuses.' But notwithstanding the fact that the type of bath employed at the present day resembles, in point of dryness of atmosphere, that of ancient Rome, the name of Turkish bath, originally given to it by Mr. Urquhart, has held good, and must now be accepted as the correct modern designation.

Neither the term "Turkish," however, nor the designation "hot-air" bath, convey to the uninitiated any idea of the true principle of "the bath," as I shall hereinafter call it for brevity's sake. More properly it is a "*heat* bath"—a *thermal cure*. In the ordinary hot-air bath, the heated air is simply a medium; and, as I have endeavoured to explain in the body of this little work, the heat is best supplied to the body of the bather by direct radiation. By the "Turkish bath," therefore, I would be understood to mean a method of supplying pure heat—not necessarily hot air—to the surface of the human body for hygienic, remedial, and curative purposes. [1]

In the following pages, however, I have, in this respect, treated of the subject from the broadest point of view, and have explained the method of designing the *hot-air bath* pure and simple, looking upon the convected and [Pg 6] radiating heat principles as both good of their kind, and perfectly admissible modes of applying heat to the human frame. I have adhered to this plan throughout, because, even supposing that it were shown conclusively to-morrow, that the principle of heating by convection is absolutely wrong, baths of this type would, owing to the slow march of improvement in this country, still be built and require to be planned. Moreover, it has been in the past, and still is, the generally accepted idea that the Turkish bath is a hot-air bath pure and simple.

Medical men of eminence who have studied the question have thought fit to retain the term "hot air" in descriptions of the Turkish bath. In deference to their opinion I may hereinafter, in places, speak of the *hot-air bath*. The arguments put forward in favour of radiant heat, with a comparatively cool atmosphere, in the sudorific chambers, are, for the most part, the result of my own experience and study.

I treat of my subject in two sections, dealing with public and private baths respectively. Chapters II. to VII. are devoted to the elucidation of the principles to be observed in the building of public baths, either for true public purposes or as commercial speculations. It is unnecessary to speak of these two classes of baths under separate heads: what is required of the one is required of the other. The only difference is that one is the property of the people, and may be required to be designed in a block of buildings containing other kinds of baths; and the other is owned by a company of persons or by a single individual as the [Pg 7] case may be, and is generally an establishment complete in itself.

It is not to the credit of the English nation that so little has been done in connection with Turkish bath building for the people. The attention given to the question of supplying bath-houses of any kind is of the most meagre character. The provisions of the Public Baths and Wash-houses Act are entirely inadequate. In these matters the German nation is far ahead of us. Fortunately for the general health, the Englishman is renowned for his morning "tub." But the cold tub is merely a tonic bath, and the Turkish bath cleanses both the inward and outward man, besides constituting a most perfect tonic. The cleanliness of the vast body of the English depends on the warm shallow bath, an ineffective means at the best, and, often, when taken at a high temperature, fraught with a real danger to certain constitutions. Used, as customary, without a tonic application of cold water, it is eminently conducive to cold-catching. But one cannot blame the average Englishman for his neglect of the health-giving habit of scientific bathing, unless he sees the advantage of, and has means to afford, a Turkish bath in his own house. He looks in vain for an appropriate, comfortable, and attractive bath-house provided for him by the Legislature, and he dislikes the thought of the impure atmosphere and odours of the so-called "Turkish baths" provided by enterprising business men. He can do nothing but fall back on his warm water bath and cold morning tub.

In the second section, comprised in Chapters VIII. to X., I have dealt with private baths, including the [Pg 8] bath in the house and mansion, in institutions of one kind and another, and in connection with training stables. In the chapter on the bath in the private house, will be found plans of baths of several types, from the smallest and least expensive to the most elaborate and costly.

It is my hope that this little work may lead to some attention being bestowed on the question of providing public Turkish baths worthy of the country; that it may add a stimulus to the building of high-class baths as commercial speculations; and that, from its pages, those desirous of experiencing the luxury of a model Turkish bath in their own homes, may learn the best methods of its design and construction. [Pg 9]

CHAPTER II.

THE GENERAL REQUIREMENTS OF A PUBLIC BATH.

In order to avoid unnecessary expense in working and management, a public Turkish bath should be convenient and *compact* in plan. It should be as perfect as possible in regard to heating and ventilation, in order to insure patronage; and, for the same reason, it should be made a thing of beauty. A badly-ventilated, inconvenient, and ill-adorned bath does harm, both to the bather and the cause. It is its own enemy, and harmful also to all other baths; whereas every ably-designed bath has in itself the elements of success, and assists existing institutions by increasing the number of converts to the process.

A good bath does not necessarily mean an elaborate and expensive one, but primarily one where the heating and ventilation are on the latest and most approved principles, and where the shampooing and washing rooms are kept sweet and clean, the bathing appliances effective, and the cooling rooms ample, and supplied with an abundance of fresh air. This is not the result of sumptuousness and elaboration, but of pure applied science. Amplitude of space, however, facilitates its [Pg 10] attainment, as it is difficult to render a cramped bath beneficial and attractive.

By an attractive bath, I would be understood to mean one in which the visitor will feel interest in the design; where pleasant objects are presented to his eye, both in the sudorific chambers and in the cooling rooms. Artistic decorations have here a commercial value. The bath requiring time, the bather is compelled to pass some hours in the various apartments, and it is therefore highly desirable that his surroundings be rendered pleasant and entertaining. In a Turkish bath, as in other architectural matters, this is not the result of a prodigal expenditure on costly decorations and fittings, but rather of a careful arrangement of necessary and desirable features, and a knowledge of the methods of obtaining piquancy of effect by their distribution on the plan.

The arrangement of the modern bath is modified from that of the Ancients and Orientals to suit the accepted form of practice in this country, so that the order of the different processes through which the bather passes governs the disposition of the various apartments. The chief object to be attained is to induce a more or less vigorous perspiration by the application of heat. This heat is now generally applied through the medium of the air, which is raised to a high temperature by being passed over and in contact with the heated surfaces of stoves of various designs, or by direct radiation from hot metal or firebrick. Theoretically, the generally-adopted method of applying the heat to the bather might be greatly improved, but practically it has been [Pg 11] found the best. Into these questions, however, I shall enter when treating of the heating and ventilating of the bath. For the present, it will suffice to say that the chief object to be attained in the bath is the supplying of an abundance of *pure hot air* to the various sudorific chambers, and the rapid withdrawal of the foul air and exhalations.

Since the disposition of the various apartments is governed by the methods of bathing in vogue, it will be necessary to first give the reader a brief account of the various processes undergone by the bather. The object of the profuse perspiration to be attained is twofold—(1) To cleanse the blood of impurities; and (2) to loosen the dead scales of the epidermis, or scarf-skin, that spreads itself everywhere over the true skin or cuticle. Besides this, however, physiologists tell us that the heat itself has a beneficial effect on the body in other ways, and is, in cases of disease, a most powerful curative and remedial agent. This latter fact explains the necessity for the high temperatures employed, as mere perspiration could be attained with a comparatively low degree of heat.

The course of treatment to be undergone by the bather, as given by Sir Erasmus Wilson, is—(1) Exposure of the naked body to hot dry air. (2) Ablution with warm and cold water. (3) Cooling and drying the skin. In addition to these, however, there should be added the process of "massage" or shampooing before washing.

The perspiration is attained in the various hot rooms—the *Tepidarium, Calidarium,* and *Laconicum*. The [Pg 12] nature of these apartments—which I shall hereinafter consider in detail—must be determined by the pretensions of the establishment.

Perspiration having been induced, the bather submits to the kneading of the muscles of the trunk and limbs by the shampooer. For this operation, which restores tone and vigour to the muscular and nervous system, a separate and distinct apartment should, in high class baths, be provided. Vigorous friction with a coarse glove succeeds the shampooing. This detaches the dead portions of the epidermis, and is an operation generally practised in the *Lavatorium*—a washing room adjoining the shampooing room. In the same place the bather receives copious ablutions with warm water. The less robust conclude the cleansing process with a douche, needle, spray, or shower bath, graduated from warm to cold; and the strong bather, by plunging into a bath of cold water, the object of which is to contract and close the sweat-glands and pores of the skin that have been swelled and opened by the high temperatures of the calorific apartments. For these purposes a small room, with the various appliances named, and a large chamber containing a more or less ample plunge bath, must be provided. In small baths, provision for both these operations is made in one general shampooing and washing room, where the bather is "massed," rubbed down, washed, and takes the plunge or shower bath. The plunge may, if thought advantageous, be placed partly in the cool apartment and partly in the hot rooms, in which case, the bather dives under a glazed partition of some sort, which, furnished with an india-rubber flap [Pg 13] dangling in the water, prevents the hot air of the sudatorium from entering the cooling rooms.

The above description gives an outline of the cleansing and hygienic processes, and of the nature of the requirements of those portions of the bath devoted to their attainment. I have named them first as being the most indispensable portion of the necessary suite of rooms, since the bath may exist if it be merely in the form of an old Irish "sweating-house," or a somewhat similar construction of the North American Indian; but without the heated chamber and its appurtenances there can be no bath.

The next important features to be considered are the dressing and cooling rooms. Before entering the bath rooms proper, the bather must divest himself of his clothing, and assume the bathing garment. The dressing room or *Apodyterium,* and the cooling room or *Frigidarium,* are generally made one and the same; but they may, with advantage, be designed as separate and distinct apartments, the provision for dressing and undressing consisting of a room or rooms with small dressing-boxes around it. The frigidarium will then be a simple apartment designed for the economical reception of the reposing couches, it being absolutely essential that the bather rest awhile, after the bath, to allow the body to gradually assume its normal temperature. Neglect of this precaution may cause a renewal of perspiration, and possibly a "cold."

If a combined apodyterium and frigidarium be adopted, it must be fitted with a number of divans to accommodate a given number of persons, or be divided [Pg 14] into smaller spaces with dwarf screens, each space receiving a pair of couches. The divisions may be effected by more or less elaborate and ornamental wooden partitions. In ladies' baths more privacy must be observed. Each lady bather should have a private dressing and reposing room, even if only formed by dwarf wooden partitions.

An arrangement may be designed whereby the bather enters first a room fitted with a number of dressing-boxes, and then passes through the frigidarium on his way to the hot rooms, whence he returns after his bath. Where the establishment is on a large scale, the arrangement may lead the bather first to a room fitted with dressing-boxes, then to the hot rooms, and finally, by way of the plunge bath, into a commodious and separate cooling room.

Subsidiary to the cooling and dressing rooms should be others for the attendants, manager, and also for the hairdresser and chiropodist, or, at any rate, some sort of provision made for them. A pay office, with counter and a set of lockers for the receipt of the bather's watch, money, and other valuables, should be the first object that one meets on entering from the vestibule connecting the establishment with the street. In connection with this office may be the manager's room, and provision for the supply of refreshments. If the bath be the property of a company, a board room may be required. As on entering a bath the visitor must immediately divest himself of his boots and shoes, in order that he may not pollute apartments that are devoted to the attainment of that cleanliness which is [Pg 15] next to godliness, a raised step must be provided at the entrance to the apodyterium to warn him to enter unshod, or a portion of the combined cooling and dressing room may be divided off by similar means. Provision for the boots and shoes must be in the form of a set of pigeon-holes near the entrance, where, also, racks for coats and hats must be placed.

The hair-dressing room and accommodation for the chiropodist—if he does not practise his art at the couch of the bather—must adjoin the frigidarium, as also should the attendants' room. A lavatory must be placed in the frigidarium when used as the dressing room. Closet accommodation should be accessible from the same apartment, but should be perfectly cut off from it by means of a passage or lobby. The greatest care should be taken to prevent these conveniences from becoming offensive. Returning from the bath, the sense of smell is peculiarly sensitive, and the slightest odour is detected. The worst position for the closets is near the door by which the bather leaves the lavatorium. Defects in this point may ruin an otherwise excellent bath. If the cooling rooms and hot rooms be on separate floors, the closets may be designed off a landing on the staircase. In the separate accommodation for attendants and shampooers the same caution must be observed.

Adjoining, under, or partly under, the laconicum must be placed the heating apparatus in its chamber, with stokery and provision for fuel, &c. The stokery should be large, light, and properly ventilated, and the attendants should be able easily to communicate with the [Pg 16] stoker. Of the arrangements for heating and supplying the water to the lavatorium I shall speak in another chapter. Laundry, linen and towel rooms, and a drying room must be provided. They are important necessities, and should not be cramped in dimensions. [Pg 17]

CHAPTER III.

THE GENERAL DISPOSITION OF PLAN OF PUBLIC BATHS.

Although the process of the bath determines the position of the various apartments in relation to one another, the exact disposition of the plan must be governed by the shape of the ground to be covered, the nature of the site and surroundings, and—if the bath be constructed in an existing building—the amount of space allotted to it. The *relative* position of chamber to chamber of the sudatorium, and of the latter to the cooling rooms, must remain more or less constant; but the angle of connection with each other, their shape, proportions, and floor levels, must, together with the positions of the subsidiary apartments, be determined by the exigencies of the site, and considerations of convenience and economy. Frequently, the architect will be called upon to design a bath in a given space in the lower floors of some existing building. He may be given the ground or basement floor to make the most of as best he can. His plan is thus considerably hampered. If the site includes the basement and ground floor of an ordinary house, he may arrange the offices and cooling and dressing rooms on the ground floor; and the hot rooms, shampooing room, and bath rooms, [Pg 18] in the basement. Where possible, the hot rooms should be pushed out beyond the back wall of the houses, and lighted from the top. In cities, the hot rooms will often have to be in the actual basement. Where space is valuable a whole house may be given up to baths if the floors be made fire and heat proof. The basement may be devoted to hot rooms and shampooing rooms, the ground floor to offices and dressing rooms, and the first floor to cooling rooms. Ladies' baths, again, can be arranged on the floors above, and both baths can be heated from one apparatus. In a bath where three floors are available, the first floor may be devoted to extra cooling and dressing rooms. In inexpensive sites the bath may be all on one level. This is the most convenient arrangement, but in large cities is generally too costly. The Hammam and Savoy baths, in London, are, however, all on one level, the former being practically all above ground, and the latter constructed in the basement of an existing building.

The London Hammam was the first public Turkish bath erected in this country, and owes its existence to the fervid zeal of the late David Urquhart. It was erected in 1862, from the designs of the late Somers Clarke. The bath rooms proper are modelled on the Eastern plan, and have quite an Oriental effect, with the stars of stained glass sparkling in the sombre domed tepidarium. In this bath the office is arranged in the old building in Jermyn Street, adjoining which is the combined frigidarium and apodyterium, a structure of wood, originally intended as a temporary building only. This is covered with an open-timbered roof, and divided [Pg 19] into nave and aisles by cut-wood posts, and lighted by a clerestory. These posts form the divisions of the divans, which are separated from one another by ornamented wood partitions worked in an Eastern manner. Connected by double doors with this apartment are the hot rooms. The main room—a very moderately-heated tepidarium—is a square on plan, with splayed angles, over which rises a dome of brickwork. On either side of this square, and connected with it by the horseshoe arches supporting the dome, are transept-like apartments, used as portions of the tepidarium, similar adjuncts existing at the ends and joining on the one hand the frigidarium, and on the other a heated smoking saloon, which occupies a position corresponding to that of a Lady-chapel in this very ecclesiastical-looking plan. On either side of this saloon are two calidaria. A drying room and laundry are arranged over the smoking saloon, and w.c.'s, &c., are placed at the end of the latter apartment. In the splayed angles supporting the dome are doors leading to four apartments—two used as hot rooms of different temperatures, and the others as a washing-room and a shampooer's waiting room. Under the dome there is an extensive platform of marble slabs, beneath which is the douche room, reached by a short flight of steps. The plunge bath is placed, partly in the tepidarium, and partly in the frigidarium, with an arrangement to prevent the transmission of the hot air, such as I have herein before explained. In the centre of the frigidarium is a little marble fountain. One of the divans is partitioned off for the accommodation of the chiropodist. A gallery is provided for the hair [Pg 20] dresser, and connected with a shop in Jermyn Street.

The ground sloping considerably, a descent of a few steps has to be made to reach the frigidarium from the street. A refreshment bar is placed in the frigidarium. The manager's room is on the second floor, adjoining the old building, and has a window overlooking the frigidarium.

The Hammam was the first public Turkish bath erected in this country, and the Savoy (Fig. 1) is one of the latest and largest, and also on one level. It was designed by Mr. C. J. Phipps, F.S.A., to suit the basement of an existing building. Entering from Savoy Hill, a short passage conducts to a staircase leading to the vestibule, where are provided rails for hats and coats. The counter of the ticket-office is placed at the entrance to the frigidarium, and near this office is the committee room—the bath being the property of a private company. In vaults projecting under the street, provision is made for an engine and dynamo. The frigidarium serves also as the apodyterium, and is cut up into divans by ornamental wood partitions. Connected with it is a saloon for the hairdresser and chiropodist, and an attendants' room. A lavatory is provided in a recess. Access is gained to the hot rooms through double doors. The plunge bath is placed partly in the hot rooms and partly in the frigidarium. The tepidarium is divided by arcades into miniature nave and aisles. Two subdivisions at the end of the tepidarium lead to the calidarium, adjoining which is the heating apparatus, fitted with two of Messrs. Constantine's "Convoluted" stoves. Access to the stokery is gained by a passage at the end of the tepidarium. [Pg 21] The shampooing room is placed off the cooler end of the tepidarium, dwarf walls separating it from the latter apartment, as also from the lavatorium. Here, there are six marble basins, corresponding with the six marble slabs in the shampooing room. A small chamber is screened off the lavatorium to accommodate the douche and spray. A passage leads from the douche room to the attendants' room, by way of the laundry. Off this passage, and approached by doors from two of the divans, are the w.c.'s, &c., for the bathers' use. Provision for the supply of refreshments is made at the back of the office. This bath is designed in an Eastern style. [Pg 22]

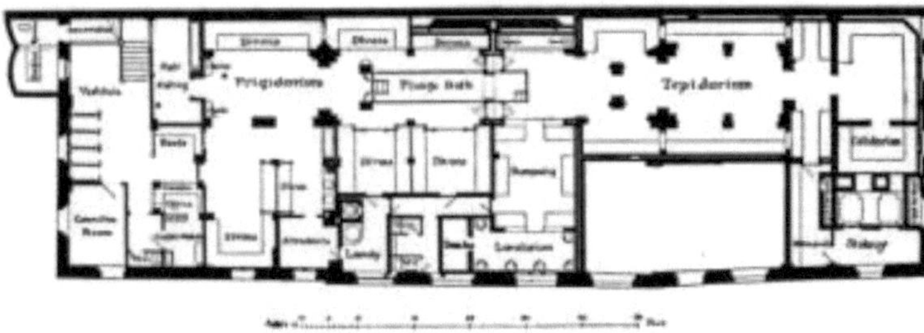

Fig. 1.
—Plan-of the-Savoy-Turkish-Baths—
Turkish Baths, Savoy Hill, London.
View larger image

In the generality of modern baths, the frigidarium forms also the apodyterium. This arrangement is economical of space, and has been found, in practice, the most convenient for bathers; but there is much to be said in favour of a separate and distinct cooling room, such as that at the Camden Town Turkish Baths. Erected from the designs of Mr. H. H. Bridgman, F.R.I.B.A., these baths are specially noteworthy for their spacious frigidarium and ample plunge bath. Entering from the street, a corridor conducts to a short flight of stairs leading to the office. Adjoining this is an apodyterium, fitted with two ranges of dressing-boxes, one above the other, a gallery forming the floor of the upper tier. From hence a short staircase leads to the door of the tepidarium, at right angles to which is the calidarium. Adjoining the tepidarium is a combined shampooing and washing room, a door in which opens into a chamber containing a plunge bath of quite [Pg 23] exceptional dimensions. A staircase leads to the door of the lofty and spacious cooling room. This is lighted from the top, and contains a fireplace, a feature usually omitted in cooling rooms, and really superfluous, though adding greatly to cheerfulness of aspect in the winter. From this frigidarium the bather can return to his dressing-box by way of a lobby. Thus he makes a complete round, and does not meet the incoming bathers on the staircase to the tepidarium.

The latest built elaborate commercial baths in London are those of Messrs. Nevill in Northumberland Avenue (Fig. 2). They were designed by Mr. Robert Walker, F.R.I.B.A., and comprise both ladies' and gentlemen's baths, though, as at the old Pompeian *Balneæ*, the former set are ungallantly cramped into a very small space. They occupy a corner site, and the entrance to the gentlemen's bath is formed at the rounded angle. In the vestibule is the usual cashier's office, and provision for hats and coats. From the vestibule the combined cooling and dressing room is entered, after passing the boot room on the left and the refreshment bar on the right. Between the boot room and the staircase is the hairdresser's room. Dwarf wooden partitions divide the cooling room. Off a landing on the staircase are a lavatory and w.c.'s and toilet-table. The staircase leads to the first floor—where are provided extra couches—and to the bath rooms in the basement. The first floor is practically a gallery. In the basement are three hot rooms, the tepidarium being an elegant apartment elaborately adorned with marbles and rich faïence. A heated smoking room adjoins the second hot room. [Pg 24] There are in this bath three shampooing rooms—an arrangement conducing greatly to privacy. A douche room and plunge bath are provided in the angle of the building. Vaults under the street are utilised as a laundry, attendants' room, meter room, and engineer's shop, and as store-rooms. [Pg 25]

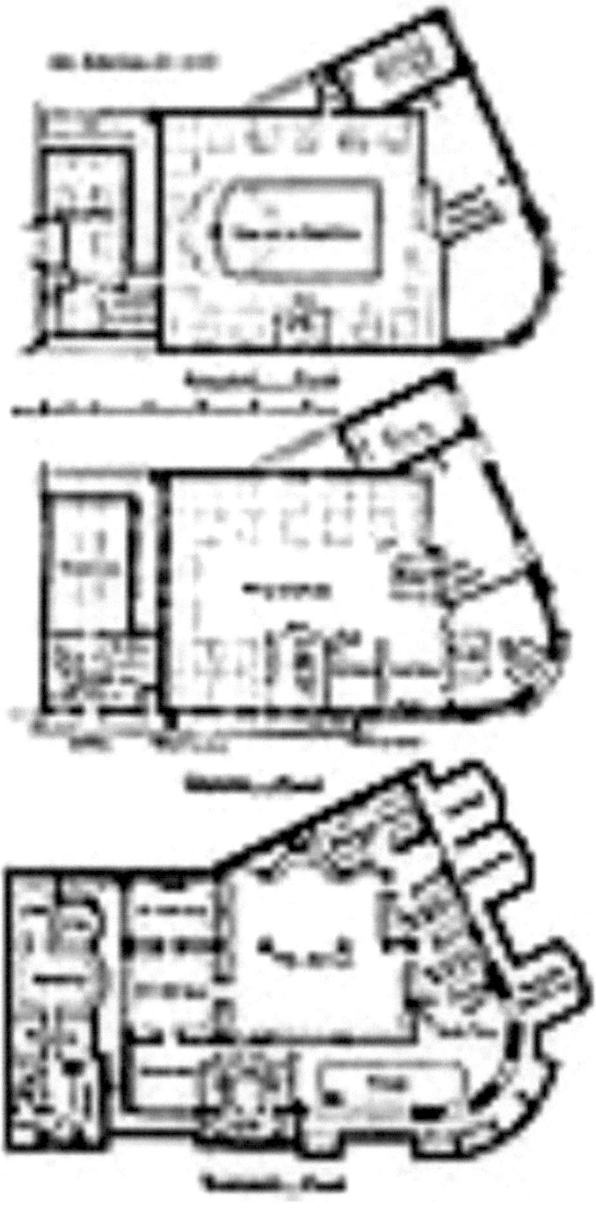

Fig. 2.

Turkish Baths, Northumberland Avenue, Charing Cross.
View larger image

The ladies' baths partly adjoin the gentlemen's, and are partly separated by an area. They are entered from the side street. On the ground floor is the pay-office and cooling room. Additional couches are provided on the first floor, where is also an attendants' room. In the basement are three hot rooms and two shampooing rooms. A washing room, shower bath, and plunge bath adjoin the shampooing rooms. The hottest rooms of both sets of these baths are within a few feet of each other. Each, however, has its separate and distinct furnace. A passage formed by the area allows access to the stokery and furnace chambers.

In Messrs. Nevill's baths at London Bridge the cooling rooms, &c., are in the basement, and the bath rooms proper in a sub-basement.

Bartholomew's baths at Leicester Square are an excellent example of a compactly-arranged double set of baths. The various apartments are designed one above the other on different floors, the area of the building being limited. On the ground floor, as usual, are the pay office and a combined cooling and dressing room, and an attendant's room. In the basement are the bath rooms, arranged *en suite*—first a shampooing and washing room, containing, also, in a very compact manner, the plunge and shower baths; next [Pg 26] is the tepidarium; then the smaller second hot room; and, lastly, the smallest hot room of a very high temperature. The heating chamber is placed adjoining this. The principle of its construction is that generally adopted in the baths erected under the late Mr. Bartholomew's direction, viz. a furnace with a coil of thin iron flue-pipes, radiating, in a measure, a certain amount of heat directly into the hot rooms. The bath rooms are divided from one another by glazed wood partitions, as distinct from the solid walls dividing baths like the Hammam and Savoy. A consideration of these two methods of dividing the hot rooms, does not, however, concern us here. A staircase from the entrance vestibule leads to the ladies' baths on the second and third floors, where also are manager's and other private rooms.

Broadly speaking, baths may be divided into two classes, viz. those in which the various apartments are arranged *en suite*, and those irregularly planned. Where possible the former arrangement is preferable, as, with the hot rooms in a line, the circulation of air is facilitated. Fig. 11 is a section of a set of hot rooms arranged *en suite*; and the baths at Figs. 24 and 25, in Chapter VIII., are planned on this principle.

As I have said above, where a basement and ground floor are available, and a little space can be gained at the back of the existing building, the office, cooling and dressing rooms can be arranged on the ground floor, and the bath rooms proper on the basement level, but with light and air above. If the site be an ordinary [Pg 27] narrow-fronted town house, and the bath an unassuming one, the plan may be arranged after the manner of Mr. Joseph Burton's baths (Fig. 3), in the Euston Road, London. Here a pair of ordinary town dwelling-houses are pressed into the service of the bath. The basement and ground floors are devoted to the baths, the upper floors forming a private hotel. On one side are the gentlemen's, and on the other, the ladies' baths. Entering the former, we find a space on the ground floor, fronting the street, serving as an office. Adjoining this is a range of dressing-boxes, and further on a cooling room, excellently lighted by a large window forming the whole end of the apartment. From this little frigidarium a marble staircase leads to the door of the tepidarium, formed at basement level at the back of the houses. This chamber is lighted by means of a ceiling-light constructed in the form of a small, flat dome, with stained-glass stars set therein. A marble seat runs round the whole of this chamber. On one side of the staircase is placed the calidarium, and, on the other, the combined shampooing room and lavatorium, a door from the latter forming an exit for the visitor who has completed his bath. At one end of the shampooing room is a chamber containing the cold plunge bath and needle bath. A door from hence leads to a staircase conducting to the furnace-chamber. A laundry is provided at the head of these stairs. The furnace-chamber is placed under the further end of the calidarium. The baths for ladies are arranged on a very similar plan. The gentlemen's baths are among the earliest erected in this country, and still form a most compact and con [Pg 28] venient institution. They were designed by Mr. James Schofield. The illustration shows the ladies' baths. The ceilings of the hot rooms are not indicated on the section.

[Pg 29]

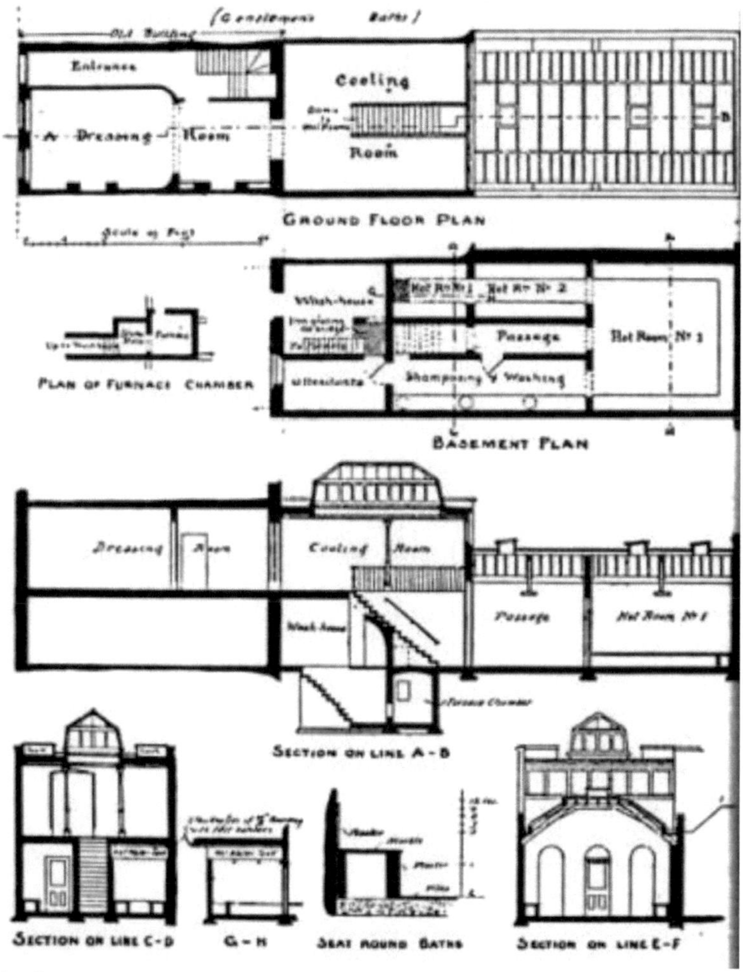

Fig. 3.
Turkish Baths, Euston Road, London.
View larger image

The whole of the baths mentioned in this chapter are the property of private individuals or companies. The number of baths provided in this country under Act of Parliament or by civic corporations is so small, and their size and design so insignificant, that it would be waste of space to describe them here. They are unworthy of the nation. One of the best is the pretty little bath provided on the first floor of the public bath-house recently erected by the Corporation of Stockport. The fine new baths at Bath erected from designs by Major Davis, the city architect, do not include a Turkish bath. It must be admitted that some slight increase in the amount of attention paid by corporate bodies to bath-building is latterly to be noticed, and a few years may possibly see a great advance in this direction. That this may indeed be so should be our sincere hope, since the lack of fine public baths is a standing disgrace to a nation that prides itself upon its cleanliness.

In Germany, considerable attention has been bestowed upon the design of the Turkish bath, many excellent baths having been built in the more complete bath-houses of the Empire. Well-arranged Turkish baths are to be found in the baths at Nuremberg, Hanover, and Bremen, the latter planned with both a first and second class frigidarium to the one set of bath rooms. The plan, however, has nothing to recommend it, and in this [Pg 30] country would be useless. The Nuremberg bath is handsomely planned, and has a spacious frigidarium. It is placed in a building comprising ladies' and gentlemen's swimming baths, shallow baths, and a Russian bath. In many of the hydropathic establishments (*Kurbäder*) of Germany, will be found excellent Turkish baths. A sumptuous double set of bath rooms is provided in the *Friedrichsbad* in Baden-Baden, which was erected at a cost of about 100,000*l.* The Turkish baths are placed on the ground floor, and in other floors are provided baths of every kind. Each set of rooms for the ladies' and gentlemen's Turkish baths comprises undressing room and cooling room, two sudorific chambers, shampooing room, douche room with cold plunge bath, and a separate chamber with warm plunge. Adjoining the shampooing room are the warm and hot rooms of the Russian bath. Between the two sets of bath rooms is placed a handsome circular swimming-bath, and adjoining, the *Wildbad*—a deep, full bath of warm mineral water.

One of the most elaborate Turkish baths erected, in modern times, is that on the Praterstern, at Vienna, which cost, in round numbers,

125,000*l*. The building comprises ladies' and gentlemen's Turkish and Russian baths, and includes a residential block for those taking a course of baths. The whole of the arrangements are on a most sumptuous scale. The cooling room of the gentlemen's baths measures no less than 35.3 metres long, and 10.5 broad. There are both warm and cold plunge baths, besides a fine circular [Pg 31] *piscina,* in a circular domed chamber. Similar provisions are made for the ladies on a smaller scale. Though plain and somewhat heavy in external design, the building internally is resplendent with tiles, marble, and ornamental woodwork. [Pg 32]

CHAPTER IV.

A DETAILED CONSIDERATION OF FEATURES PECULIAR TO THE BATH.

It is scarcely necessary to say anything more as to the subsidiary apartments of a Turkish bath. Such adjuncts as the entrance hall and vestibule, the pay office, refreshment department, laundry and drying-rooms, hairdressing and attendants' rooms, and other minor provisions, are obviously simple matters, requiring little or no detailed explanation. Sufficient has already been said about them to enable the architect, assisted by the drawings given, to design them with convenience and economy. The features peculiar to the bath are those requiring careful consideration. It is upon the design of the hot rooms, the cooling rooms, and the washing rooms that the success or non-success of a new bathing establishment depends, and too much study cannot be given to these apartments.

The Sudorific Chambers.

These are now generally required in a suite of three—"first, second, and third hot." The first is the tepidarium, and must be by far the largest of the three, since in it the greater number of bathers will assemble at one time. The last must be the hottest room—the laconicum—and [Pg 33] need only be a very small one, as but few bathers use it, and that, generally, for a very short time. The second hot room should be about midway, in size and temperature, between the first and the third. Of a given area allotted to the hot rooms, from one-half to two-thirds may be devoted to the tepidarium, and from one-third to one-half to the super-heated rooms, always remembering that it is well to err on the side of providing a large and roomy tepidarium. Of the space allowed for the smaller rooms, one-quarter to one-third may be given to the hottest, and the remaining space to the second hot-room, or calidarium.

The hot rooms, it should be remembered, are strictly bath rooms, and must be treated as such; that is to say, the whole of the floors, walls, ceilings, partitions, and fittings, must be capable of being frequently cleansed with water. The choice of materials to be employed for lining the walls, &c., is therefore limited. And in two ways. For not only must they be of this washable nature, but they must be of a character to resist the influence of the heat. Happily, this is an age of glazed-ware and vitrified goods of every description. Glazed and fire-burnt bricks and tiles, terracottas, faïence, and pottery generally, are now so extensively manufactured that there is little excuse for not constructing a bath throughout of materials at once washable and unaffected by high temperatures. Still, in baths where rigid economy must be studied, and lowness of cost is the great object, *plaster* may be placed upon the walls of the hot rooms, and in its way will answer admirably, and be fairly washable. It has even one advantage—it [Pg 34] does not become unbearably hot to the touch, should the bather lean against the walls, whereas, with a highly glazed surface the walls become burning hot, and need lining with a dado of felt or other non-conducting substance. And since this latter method overcomes the objection named, the best possible material for lining the walls is glazed brickwork. In cases where elaboration is desired, they may be lined with marbles and faïence. With a judicious selection of colours, however, a very pleasing appearance can be given by the employment of simple glazed brickwork, and at a very moderate cost.

The flooring in cheap baths is admirably formed by simple unglazed tile pavement over concrete. A slight roughness is very agreeable to the feet. Glazed tiles are inadmissible, as they become too hot for the naked feet; and if the slightest moisture come upon them they are rendered dangerously slippery. In elaborate baths, marble, and marble mosaics may be used, but the surface must not be too smooth. In providing floorings, the greatest care should be taken to avoid anything liable to become slippery to the tread.

Floors of ordinary-sized baths, where the soil is reliable, may be of 6 in. of concrete, with mosaics or tiles laid in cement. The benches for reclining and shampooing must be built up from this with half-brick risers and glazed fronts, having weathered marble slabs with rounded nosings, as illustrated at Fig. 3.

The ceilings of the fire and heat-proof floors, which, when there are other apartments above, *must* be provided over the hot rooms, may be of plaster. But the heat at the ceiling level is very great, and the plaster here [Pg 35] rapidly darkens and blackens, and in this state looks anything but attractive in a place where the mere suspicion of uncleanliness is nauseating. If employed (and this remark also applies to plaster on walls), it should be used in the simplest manner possible, without the slightest attempt at modelling the surface. Enamelled iron may be used, with effect, for ceilings. The little laconicum is best covered with a flat vault, the soffit being of glazed bricks, and the springing being brought down below the main ceiling level.

Fire-proof floors over hot rooms may be of any design that is also heat-proof. The main point is to have a sufficient thickness of concrete, and the iron joists and cross girders well buried therein. Ordinary floors may be rendered heat-proof by partially filling the space between ceiling and floorboards with sawdust or sheets of slag-wool laid on boarding nailed to fillets on the joists. The sawdust should be filled up to the top of the joists; over this a layer of thick felt, and the boarding above. This, however, is only a makeshift when compared with a solid floor of concrete.

When the hot rooms are in a basement in the open, they may be top-lighted, and the ceiling above need not be a heavy fire-proof construction. A sufficient air space, however, must be provided between the ceiling and roof, to prevent irradiation of heat—a remark that applies also to anything in the shape of a window in the sudatorium. It must be double, or look into an area covered with pavement lights. In the case of a top-lighted room there must be a ceiling-light and a skylight. [Pg 36]

Where the hot rooms are constructed quite above ground, consideration must be given to the prevention of loss of heat by radiation. This may be effected by providing thick hollow walls, the cavity being often usefully employed for the extraction of the vitiated air.

Heat permeating other apartments and neighbouring premises is a frequent source of trouble to the builder of a Turkish bath, but is always the result of want of study of the subject on the part of the designer. The evil may be successfully combated if it be resolved that no hot room, shampooing room, or lavatorium shall be constructed without a thick concrete floor above, and that the furnace chamber be perfectly and completely insulated. Should the walls of the hot rooms adjoin apartments to which it is urgently necessary that the heat should be prevented from being transmitted, they may be rendered heat-proof by building them hollow and filling the cavity with soot.

Double doors and lobbies must be employed to prevent the transmission of the heated air to rooms where its presence would be injurious. To keep the hot air of the bath-rooms from the cooling-rooms, &c., should be the great aim of the architect. Many baths are rendered quite repulsive by what I may perhaps term the "sudorific smell" that assails the nostrils of the visitor entering the vestibule.

The space allotted to the sudatory chambers may be divided into the various rooms, either by glazed brick walls or by framed and glazed partitions; or again, they may be formed by a combination of solid brick [Pg 37] work and glazed woodwork. Any piers in these rooms must be of brickwork, iron columns being inadmissible. Masonry, too, must be discarded throughout, or used with caution. Some stones—such as red Mansfield—become black with exposure to the heat, and others fare still worse. The employment of porous and absorbent materials must be guarded against throughout this portion of the bath, as it should be remembered that effete matters, particles of waste tissue, and possibly the germs of disease, are continually being given off by the perspiring bathers, and must be prevented from finding a lodgment.

The best woods for use in the hot rooms are close-grained and free from essential oils. Mahogany is excellently adapted for the purpose, and so, also, is teak. Pitch pine must be discarded altogether. Deal, when employed, should be perfectly seasoned, and may then give trouble from the exudation of turpentine.

The partitions, and the doorways in them, must be so placed as to govern the flow of hot air. So long as the main divisions be planned with this end in view, the separate rooms may be divided and broken up as the architect may fancy. But the constant flow of the heated air from the inlet in the hottest room towards the lavatorium must not be interfered with by recesses, nooks, and corners, or anything that would cause the current to stagnate. And here we may see the practical advantage possessed by a bath where the hot rooms are *en suite,* and in a line with one axis. For here the air sweeps uninterruptedly through the different [Pg 38] chambers without eddying around corners and stagnating in recesses far out of the main stream.

The doorways in the partitions should not be too lofty. They should not be hung with doors, as anything necessary in this way will be amply supplied by depending curtains.

Glazing in the hot rooms requires care. The glass will expand considerably with the heat, and, what is more, if the furnace fire die out rapidly at any time, will contract and fracture. This difficulty, however, is the result of bad management, and does not concern the architect, unless, indeed, it be the result of improper fixing. Even moderate-sized sheets of glass should be carefully fixed in chamois leather with screwed beading, *putty* being wholly inadmissible. The sheets of glass should not be of too large dimensions. Rolled glass will be found the cheapest in the end, as inferior qualities, where homogeneity of texture is wanting, will crack and split in all directions. Lead glazing should be altogether discarded.

No provision for draining the hot rooms is necessary, as they must, when in use, be kept free from moisture. The floor may, however, if thought desirable, be laid with an imperceptible fall the way the water would be swept when cleansing—viz. towards the lavatorium.

As the best position for a bather to assume in the sudatorium is one approaching to the horizontal, a bath cannot be considered complete unless a liberal number of marble-slabbed benches be provided. These should run round the solid walls, the risers of the benches being formed of brickwork—glazed, faced with tiles, or [Pg 39] plastered—and white marble slabs set thereon. These slabs cannot be less than 24 in. wide, and must be of the ordinary seat height—not lower. In the risers must be provided a liberal number of "hit-and-miss" ventilator gratings, the vitiated air finding its way from the space beneath the slabs in the way designed, which may be into surrounding areas, into hollow walls, or into a flue or flues running the whole height of the building.

The air at the floor line and that at the ceiling level being of vastly different temperatures, it follows that an arrangement might be designed whereby the benches might be stepped in three or four rows, and, by ascending, the bather could select any temperature he might choose. Such an arrangement was often employed in the baths of the ancient Romans, and has been tried in modern institutions; but it should be avoided. The expirations from the lungs and the exudations from the bodies of the bathers *fall*, and it therefore follows that all below the first tier would be breathing air polluted by those above them. The system, therefore, stands condemned.

As regards height, the sudorific chambers should not be too lofty, or they cannot, on the ordinary hot-air plan, be heated with due economy. The vastness of the old Roman tepidarium would have been impracticable under this system; but with the heat radiating direct from the walls and the floors, there was no difficulty. It is far better to have a comparatively low chamber with a constant stream of freshly-heated air passing through it, than a lofty one with a sluggish current. From 10 to 15 or [Pg 40] 16 ft. may be taken as moderate extremes of height in a public bath. The small third hot room will be less lofty if the heating-chamber be placed under it; for by raising the floor of the laconicum a few feet, so as to necessitate ascending to it by a few steps from the level of the tepidarium, one can more economically construct the furnace chamber.

This latter, which I have more particularly described and illustrated in the chapter on heating and ventilation, should, if the system adopted be on the ordinary hot-air principle, be so placed that an abundant supply of fresh pure cold air can be obtained for the furnace, which, when heated, can be delivered into the hottest room above, not less than 5 ft. from the level of the floor of that chamber, and, also, where a smoke flue of ample section can be constructed. The heated air may be delivered through the gratings in the walls of the laconicum, or a shaft of glazed brickwork, of rectangular section, may be constructed against the end wall and coped at the required level—5 ft. or more above the floor line. Should the exigencies of the site separate the furnace chamber from immediate connection with the hottest room, the heated air must be conducted from the former to the latter by means of a large shaft or shafts of glazed brickwork. Similar means may have to be employed to bring the cold air to the heating-chamber, and at the mouth of this shaft some provision must be made for filtering the air before it is brought into contact with the heating surfaces of the furnace.

Horizontal and inclined flues for conducting hot or cold air may be carried from point to point on rolled [Pg 41] iron joists having tooled York slabs set thereon, the flues being constructed of 4½ in. brickwork with glazed face internally, and covered with tooled York slabs. Provision must be made, in such flues, for effective cleansing, by means of iron air-tight doors.

The Lavatorium and Shampooing Room.

The lavatorium and shampooing room now engage our attention. In elaborate baths they may, for the sake of effect, be distinct apartments, while, where strict economy must be studied, they may be comprised in one room; and where, again, space is extremely valuable, the plunge bath and douche may be also included. If the first arrangement be adopted, the shampooing room must be connected with the tepidarium, and the lavatorium placed next. Where the combination apartment is used, it will take the position of the shampooing room. Practically, the combination arrangement is the best. It is putting the bather to needless and undesirable trouble to require him to move from one apartment to another during the washing process.

The suite of washing and shampooing rooms may be arranged in either one of the following ways, according to the pretensions and requirements of the establishment:—(1) A shampooing room, a lavatorium, a douche room, and a plunge bath chamber; (2) a combined shampooing and washing room, and a combined douche and plunge bath chamber; (3) several small combined shampooing and washing rooms, a douche room, and a plunge bath chamber; (4) an apartment comprising [Pg 42] shampooing slabs, washing basins, douche, &c., and a plunge bath.

A single shampooing room does not present a very complicated problem to the designer. The chief object to be borne in mind is that the shampooers require "elbow-room," and their patient in a convenient position to allow of their practising their art. As this is no light task—if properly performed—it becomes of urgent moment that the apartment should be no less perfectly ventilated than a sudorific chamber. In a vitiated atmosphere, no shampooer can work well for a prolonged period, and, moreover, pure air is as necessary for the bathers when in these places, as when they are in the hot rooms.

The shampooing benches may be similar in description and size to those in the hot rooms. A width of 2 ft. is an ample provision, since the shampooer can more conveniently work with the bather as near him as possible. The benches may be constructed in a similar manner to those before described. They must be arranged on plan so that the shampooer has ample room, whilst at the same time space is not extravagantly wasted. The benches must be topped with white marble slabs. They may run round the wall, or be placed at right angles to them; or, again, if found more convenient, they may be altogether isolated. Similar means of ventilating the shampooing and washing rooms as the hot rooms must be provided. The vitiated air must be extracted at the floor level, as the temperature here must be maintained considerably above that of respired air.

Movable wooden-framed marble-topped benches may [Pg 43] be substituted for those of a permanent type; but the plan has nothing to recommend it except lowness of cost.

The separate lavatorium need not be so large as its adjoining shampooing room, as here the bathers will not recline, but sit or stand before washing-basins, to which must be conducted the flow pipes of hot water, and branches from the cold water supply pipe. These basins—which may be of glazed earthenware if solid marble cannot be afforded—should be large and capacious. Of water-fittings I shall speak under the head of "Appliances."

In a combined shampooing and washing room the benches and basins will be required together. The basins may be fixed under a hole in the marble slabs, or affixed to the walls, as may be convenient. Whilst arranging the position of the benches with regard to the room, and the basins with regard to the benches, it will be as well to remember the postures that the bather assumes whilst being shampooed—viz. 1st, sitting; 2nd, on the back; 3rd, reverse. The basin must be so placed with respect to the slab that the shampooer may, without altering his position, take water from the basin with his handbowl, and pour it over the bather. A shampooer cannot well work with less than 5 ft. 6 in. between his slab and that of his adjoining fellow, when the slabs are at right angles to the wall and the adjoining shampooer is also working in the same space between the two benches. Where the room is long and a row of benches are placed at right angles to the wall, the shampooers have each their separate space to work in. Each one can then [Pg 44] manage in 4 ft., and the slabs can be set out 6 ft. from centre to centre. Where the long sides of the slabs are against the walls and the basins are sunk into the slabs, there must be at least 7 ft. 6 in. from basin to basin. In the case of slabs at right angles to the walls, the basins are best placed between the slabs.

It is an excellent plan to provide a slight screen in one corner of the washing room, behind which the entering bather may, if he chooses, have a warm spray from a large rose before proceeding to the hot rooms.

In ladies' baths it is well to provide private shampooing recesses by means of partitions of sufficient height, which may be of wood and obscure glass. In this way any shampooing room may be rendered more private. Upright marble slabs will often be found useful in dividing the benches.

The walls and ceilings of the apartments now under consideration may, so long as there be a dado of glazed ware, be lined in the same way as the hot rooms. But as regards flooring, still more care is required to prevent slipperiness. The soap and water that will be plentifully spilt around, renders this precaution needful. Moreover, provision must be made for drainage.

The flooring may be of rough tile mosaic, or simple tiles. Marble is too slippery, and glazed tiles are wholly inadmissible. Marble mosaics, roughly set, may be employed. The fall to which the floor is laid must be determined by the position of the gullies.

The drainage system of a hot-air bath is a most important consideration. In a place where the occupants are, literally, *breathing at every pore*, it is obvious that [Pg 45] too much care cannot be taken to prevent all possible odours, and the slightest suspicion of an escape of deleterious sewer gases. The traps employed in the washing rooms should be of the best possible design and material, and proof against the evil known as "siphoning." The gullies above them are best placed adjoining one of the ventilators in the walls, at the floor level, as then a current of air sweeps over them and up the extraction flues. It is not always that an opportunity is afforded to cut off the waste water from the drainage; where the bath rooms are above ground, however, this should be done if practicable. Where possible, an excellent plan is to construct a culvert under the basement floor. In this the whole of the pipes can be placed—the soil-pipes, the lavatorium and plunge bath wastes, &c., and access gained to them by a manhole. By this means a cut-off could be effected between waste-pipes and the sewerage system. The culvert itself could be ventilated by connecting it with an extraction flue. This is all costly; but the builder of a Turkish bath will do well to be prepared to lay out a liberal sum to perfect the system of drainage of the establishment, and in the end, when the public have appreciated the attention bestowed, he will thank his architect for having impressed upon him the necessity for this extra expenditure.

The Douche Room.

The douche room should be a small chamber adjoining the lavatorium, and fitted with a circular needle bath [Pg 46] with shower or douche above, and any other kind of spray bath that may be required. It should not be a dark, cold, uninviting hole. For this reason, and also because a corner is admirably adapted to receive an appliance of the shape of a needle bath, it is better, often, to fit it up in an angle of the lavatorium. But of these additions I shall have much to say anon, as one of the most important points about a bath is the arrangement of the water-fittings. Needle baths will be found indicated, on the plans given in these pages, by an incompleted circle.

The Plunge Bath.

Though, according to medical authorities, this does not form a *necessary* appendage to the hot-air bath, it is yet a feature that *must* be provided in the least pretentious of public establishments. Ever since, and long before, Cicero observed, in a letter to his brother Quintus, "Latiorem piscinam voluissem ubi jactata brachia non offenderentur," men who have taken the hot-air bath have loved the ample plunge. But although it should be sufficiently large for any bather to take a dive, and for an expert to take a true "header," it is a vast mistake to overdo it, and construct a small swimming bath, out of all proportion with the other features of the establishment. One does not look for such an adjunct: it is a great expense to keep up, requires a lot of space, and tempts many to stay too long in the cold water. All purposes will be served by a bath which will allow the bather to swim without touching the sides with his hands, [Pg 47] and to dive along under water without danger of striking his head at the other end before he rises to the surface. Wherever possible, the bath should be quite 25 ft. in length and at least 7 ft. wide. In inferior institutions it may be as narrow as 4 ft. and proportionately shorter; but in such a bath one can only flounder about, and healthy bathers will go elsewhere.

In deciding the position of the plunge bath there is one point to be strongly guarded against, and that is, that it be not stowed away in a damp, cold-looking, cellar-like place. Such a position may be all very well when the proprietor wishes to conceal dirty water; but from every other point of view it is highly objectionable. The wise man will bring his bath forward into the lightest possible position, where its clear, limpid waters will look enticing instead of repelling. For preference, it should be placed where the bather will take it naturally, *en route* to the frigidarium, as at the Charing Cross baths, previously illustrated. In baths all on one level, it is convenient to place the bath partly in the lavatorium and partly in the frigidarium; but, to most persons, the necessity for passing under the inevitable partition and flap spoils the full enjoyment of the plunge. If placed within the frigidarium, and approached by a door from the lavatorium, some sort of a screen should be provided over the bath, as, at times, the apparition appearing at the above door, in full view of the occupants of the cooling-room, is somewhat ludicrous.

The demands of decency must be borne constantly in mind by the architect of a Turkish bath. If the bather, on leaving the plunge bath, finds himself in the frigi [Pg 48] darium, he must ascend the steps under hanging towels. The arrangement that will be found the most convenient—a direct importation from the East—is to suspend a hoop from the ceiling, and from this hang cords attached to towels. The hoop can be swung by an attendant over the end of the bath, and in it the bather can dry himself and be wrapped in towels before proceeding to his couch.

Whether the plunge bath be placed in a separate chamber, in the lavatorium, or partly in the frigidarium, its construction will remain essentially the same. If not in shape and size, in other respects it is a small swimming bath. The weight and pressure of the water must be remembered. A good foundation must be prepared for the bath, with a thick layer of concrete passing well under the side walls and covering the whole floor. The side walls should be built of concrete and lined with white glazed bricks. In certain soils, the excavation for the bath may be puddled with advantage, but if properly constructed, this should be unnecessary. The bottom of the bath need not be flat, as the most economical method of constructing a plunge bath is to make its deepest part about two-thirds of its length from the end at which the bather enters. This may be about 4 ft. 6 in. in depth from bottom to water-line. From this point the floor will slope towards either end, gradually towards the entering end, and more rapidly towards the exit. At either end, where the depth of water should be about 3 ft, must be provided steps for ascent and descent. If the bath be not more than 6 ft. wide, these should occupy the whole width, and be of marble or slabs of some cheaper material [Pg 49] on brick bearers, or they may be built solid. A coping of marble, stone, or purpose-made bricks must be placed on the side walls; and, if the bath be in the cooling room, this may advantageously be raised several inches to protect from splashing. On the coping may be required metal standards and a neat hand-railing. A water-supply pipe and screw-down tap, an overflow and a waste-pipe will be needed, all of which I have more particularly specified hereinafter.

The plunge bath is at times a source of two difficulties—it may leak, and it may be below the level of drain. The first evil is the result of an error in design, or of bad workmanship; the latter is unavoidable. The following method of constructing a plunge bath has been adopted with perfect success:—On the bed of concrete prepared for its floor, erect side walls of concrete, and on the floors and walls thus formed spread two distinct layers of asphalt, covering all and running up to the underside of coping. Against the sides build half-brick walls in cement, with glazed face, and lay the floor with glazed bricks flat. The general principles of this construction I show in the accompanying illustration.

Where the bath is lower than the drain, all that can be done is to drain out as much as possible and pump the remaining water from a "sump" provided in a suitable position. By raising the plunge bath chamber a few feet, the bottom of bath may, in some cases, be just kept above the drain level; but steps must then be placed between it and the washing-room, and steps in such places are dangerous, being very liable to become slippery. [Pg 50]

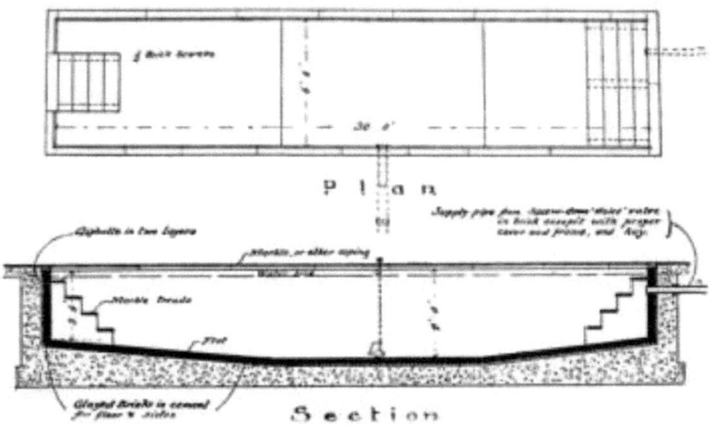

Fig. 4.
A Plunge Bath.
View larger image
[Pg 51]

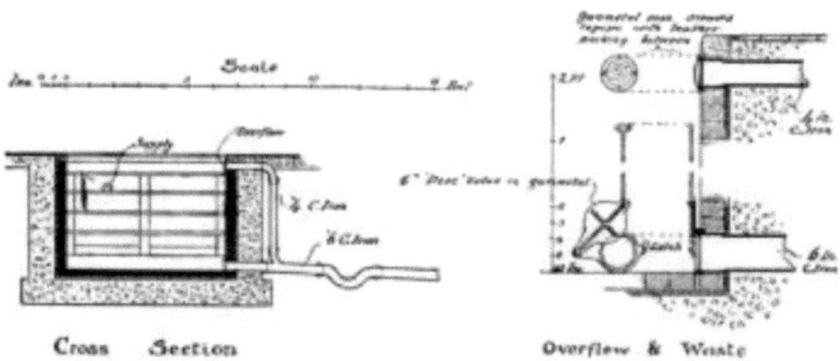

View larger image

[Pg 52]

The Frigidarium or Cooling Room, and Dressing Accommodation for Bathers.

Dressing and cooling accommodation in a public bath may be provided in one of the following ways:—1. A separate frigidarium and distinct dressing room, arranged (*a*) in direct communication with one another, or (*b*) connected by a lobby, corridor, or ante-room;—2. A combination apartment arranged (*a*) with dressing-boxes around the walls, and couches in the centre, or *vice versâ*; (*b*) with Oriental divans; (*c*) with couches screened off in pairs or singly by dwarf wood screens; (*d*) with a few private dressing-boxes, a few couches, and a few lounges, and easy cushioned chairs; and (*e*) as a simple room with couches placed therein, by the side of which the bather will undress, and on which he will recline after his bath.

The first of these arrangements may be admirably adapted to unpretentious establishments, where, however, it is wished to employ separate rooms; the second (1, *b*) is only suitable for elaborate baths of the highest class, in which it may be adopted with excellent and with practical results. Of the combination arrangements (*a*) has little to recommend it; (*b*) is expensive and extravagant of space, though it may be made very effective in appearance and very pleasing and comfortable; (*c*) is suitable for ladies' baths; (*d*) is very practicable, and gives the apartment a pleasant, homely look; and (*e*) is best for cheap baths, being the simplest [Pg 53] arrangement possible, wholly unsuited, however, to establishments of any pretension.

If the plan include a separate cooling room, it is nothing more than a spacious, cheerful apartment, designed with a view to the reception of couches, and the usual accessories designed in connection with it—the refreshment room, hairdresser and chiropodist's saloon. If this separate cooling room be provided, a distinct apodyterium, with little dressing-boxes, must be designed. If the bath be small and easily managed, curtains may be employed to screen those undressing; but if it be a large establishment, with a number of bathers constantly dressing and undressing, doors must be provided, and these must be under lock and key in charge of an attendant. Each dressing-box must be fitted with a seat, rack, and shelf; and looking-glasses, toilet-tables, and lavatories for general use must be placed in the room, which must be designed in direct connection with the frigidarium.

This should be spacious, light, lofty, and perfectly ventilated, the vitiated air being here extracted at the ceiling level, since the temperature at which the apartment will be kept is an ordinary one—*over* that of the exterior air when the weather is cold, and *under* when it is at all hot.

Where the cooling room and dressing room do not immediately adjoin, the means of communication should be carefully studied, so that it may be free from cross draughts of cold air, and so that it may be dignified and room-like—not a mere passage. It may have the air of an ante-room, but must not be crossed by entering [Pg 54] bathers who have not divested themselves of their boots or shoes. Slamming doors should be avoided, having regard to the exposed condition of the bathers.

In spite of the theoretical and sentimental advantages of separate cooling and dressing-rooms, a combined frigidarium and apodyterium seems to have found favour latterly.

Personally, I would gladly enter a protest against the employment of the combined cooling and dressing room as a decidedly uncleanly habit. It is certainly not pleasant to know that, having obtained perfect physical cleanliness, both inwardly and outwardly, one must return to couches whereon previous bathers may, as likely as not, have, however temporarily, deposited more or less of their underclothing or superimposed raiment. But economy of construction is nowadays a question that must be considered at every step, and the combination apartment saves both space and materials, and is also economical as regards attendance. Moreover, it must be confessed that a cooling room provided with elegant and spacious divans, wherein the bather dresses and undresses, may be made very pleasing to the eye and withal comfortable and convenient. The dressing-boxes, too, of the separate apodyterium are not conducive to the general sense of comfort.

In arranging the plan of a combined cooling and dressing room it is necessary to first decide as to how the apartment will be furnished—viz. which of the plans above mentioned shall be adopted. This is much a matter of individual taste, though, as I have said above, the divan is to be preferred in many cases. It is often [Pg 55] well to provide a cooling room of what may be called the "picturesque" order, or the reverse of stiff formality. By this I mean such an arrangement as 2, *d*. The bather can then choose between reclining in semi-privacy or in the open, or, again, resting in an easy chair. With a handsome plunge bath and a pretty little fountain, such rooms may be rendered very attractive.

Whatever be the plan adopted, it must, I repeat, be carefully thought out previously, and not left as an afterthought. The size of the reclining couch will be found to be the governing feature. This should be 6 ft. 6 in. long by 2 ft. 6 in. wide, or 6 ft. by 2 ft., according as luxury or economy is the end in view. Next to this must be considered the space allowed for each bather to dress in, and also the routes for bathers and attendants. Four feet between the couches is a sufficient space where couches are screened off in pairs.

Couches may be arranged in pairs or singly. *Two pairs* of couches screened off with only a small space between of 4 ft. or so is an objectional arrangement. It is difficult to explain why this is so; but the bather who has made one of four strangers thus closely penned up will appreciate the objection. An arrangement of four couches must expand into a spacious divan.

At Fig. 5 are shown different ways of arranging couches in the frigidarium. A shows the objectionable arrangement spoken of; B is the comfortable, spacious divan; C the method of placing couches in pairs; and D is a private couch suitable for ladies' baths.

The floor of a cooling room must be boarded. In a bath where cost is subordinate to excellence, a parquetry [Pg 56] floor may be provided, and mats employed, as cleaner than fixed carpets. The walls and ceilings may be treated in any manner that may be chosen—plastered, papered, or decorated with colour.

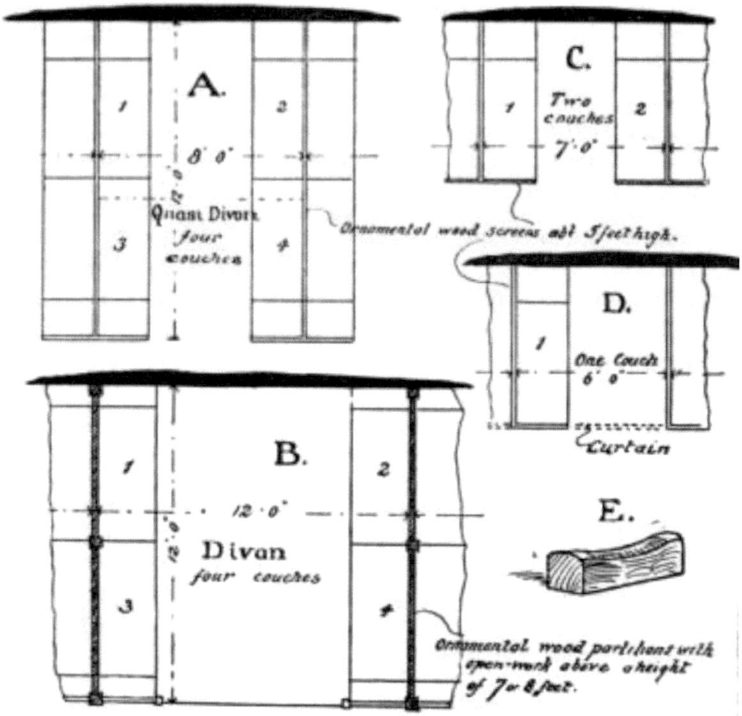

Fig. 5.
Methods of arranging Couches in Cooling Room.
View larger image

Any shaped room may be adopted as a combined frigidarium and apodyterium so long as it fulfils the [Pg 57] essential points—i.e. that it be spacious, capable of easy and perfect ventilation, and of being kept cool, light, and cheerful. In the cooling room the bather will often stay longer than in any other apartment, and no pains should be spared to render it healthy, comfortable, and attractive. The hygienic points to be attended to are, that there be an abundant supply of fresh cool air and an effective withdrawal of vitiated air; for the *cold-air bath* in the cooling room is, in its way, as all-important as the bath of hot air. The freshness of the air is of equally vital importance, as much of the *invigorating* effect of the bath—that effect which to the minds of the uninformed is *weakening*—results from submitting the heated skin to volumes of cold air. [2] In arranging any screens or screen walls in the cooling room, therefore, regard must be had to the method of ventilation, that there be no stagnant corners and recesses. The scheme of ventilation must be decided by the nature of the apartment and its position. In most cases the air is best admitted through the windows, fitted with fanlights falling backwards from the top, and extracted by a powerful self-acting exhaust at the ceiling level. In some positions extraction flues will have to be built, and, in others, flues of large area must conduct to the source from which the fresh air is drawn. Under certain circumstances perfect ventilation will not be obtainable without the aid of a powerful blowing fan- [Pg 58] wheel driven by a motor of some sort, and running so as to exhaust the vitiated air. The means does not so much matter so long as the end be gained, and an ample supply of cool air obtained. A warm, close "cooling room" is worse than useless. In such places the bather will break out into renewed perspiration, and lie perspiring for hours, and become greatly weakened thereby, with a good chance of taking a chill on leaving the establishment.

Cooling rooms will always remain sufficiently *warm* in all weathers if they be in any ordinary relation to the heated apartments; but in the height of summer care is required to keep them sufficiently cool. Where simple, everyday precautions will not suffice, the air itself must be cooled, either by passing it through a cold chamber or over ice-boxes in inlet tubes, or through a water-spray. Only in exceptional cases, however, is it necessary to resort to such measures, as, contrary to the teachings of theorists, it has been found in practice that the proper temperature for the cooling room of a hot-air bath varies in different states of the weather, and should not remain constant all the year round. [Pg 59]

CHAPTER V.

HEATING AND VENTILATION.

Of the many questions that merit attention and study in connection with the Turkish bath, all sink into insignificance by the side of that of the *heating* and the *nature of the heat* supplied in the sudatory chambers. Other things being equal, it is, after all, the *heating* that distinguishes one bath from another on the score of excellence. The heating of the "bath" is the Alpha and Omega of the whole matter.

There are two ways in which heat may be applied to the body—by direct radiation, as from the sun or an open fire; and by convection, as through a volume of air.

The ancient Roman bathers, with floors below them which rested upon *pilæ*, or little pillars of brick or tile, around which the flames and hot gases from the furnace played, and surrounded by heated, hollow walls, evidently submitted themselves to the action of a heat that must have been of a purely radiating character.

So, also, in a less perfect manner, the Turks, who employ flues running beneath the floors, and the Moors, who adopt stoves visible to the bathers.

Theoretically, radiant heat in a bath is vastly superior to that which is transmitted to the body through the [Pg 60] medium of the air. Its virtues have been extolled by David Urquhart and other eminent authorities on the bath. "There is a difference," says Mr. Urquhart, "between radiating and transmitted caloric.... I cannot pretend to treat of this great secret of nature; to work out this problem a Liebig is required. This I can say, that such heat is more endurable than common heat. There is a liveliness about it which transmitted heat lacks. You are conscious of an electrical action. It is to transmitted heat what champagne is to flat beer.... Let us drop, if you please, the word 'bath': it is 'heat.' Let us away with that absurdity 'hot-air': it is the application of heat to the human frame." Elsewhere this writer has pointed out that the terms *thermæ, sèjac,* and *hammâm*—the names given to the bath by the Romans, Moors, and Orientals proper—mean *heat,* and not "hot-air" or "hot-air bath."

My own studies, observations, and experience lead me to the conclusion that the direction in which we shall improve the "Turkish bath" will be in the way of providing sudatories that shall give off pure, radiant heat in such a manner that the whole surface of the body may be sensible of a degree of heat, while the lungs may breathe comparatively cool air—air that has not passed over the sides of a fiery furnace and been suddenly raised to an enormous temperature, but which has received its heat by a gentle and gradual process of warming. Under this system the heat of which we are sensible is as the gentle Zephyr to rude Boreas or the biting eastern winds. If we go into a kiln of brickwork, such as is employed in firing clay goods, after the charge has been [Pg 61] removed and all fumes and odours have disappeared, we shall note the soft and balmy nature of the heat that radiates directly from the walls and vaulting. We are, to all practical intents and purposes, *in a Roman laconicum.* The thick walls have been highly charged with caloric during the firing of the bricks or other articles. They have absorbed vast quantities of heat, and are now giving off the same to the enclosed air and to ourselves standing within. In the old Roman bath the walls were charged with caloric by means of innumerable earthen tubes lining the sides of the laconicum, and covered with a peculiar plaster. But in both cases the nature of the resultant heat is identical. It radiates to one from all sides. There is no acrid biting of the face such as one feels in the worst type of *hot-air* baths; no unpleasant fulness or aching of the head; and no panting or palpitating. Such is the "bath" of pure radiant heat, a thing totally distinct from, and altogether of a different genus to, the bath of heated air. And one might be pardoned for the enthusiasm which would lead one to suggest that it is only in the supplying of this kind of radiant heat in the modern bath that true and rapid progress can be expected, and possibly that not until this great or partial—according as the system of radiation and convection pertains in existing baths—revolution has been effected, will the bath, at present used by the few, become the custom of the many. Some day, peradventure, this hypothetical method of employing pure radiant heat may be rendered possible and practicable, and we may be placed in a bath where we shall receive great heat whilst breathing a compara [Pg 62] tively cool atmosphere, and thus receive a measure of that electrical invigoration we experience when, in some sheltered bathing cove, we have exposed our bodies to the fiercest rays of the morning sun whilst yet we breathe the fresh, cool, ozone-laden air.

Till modern invention, however, has provided us with this desideratum in the heating of the bath, we must be satisfied with existing methods. And unless something really practical is perfected, it is far wiser to rely upon the system of heating by convection through the air—the principle, generally adopted, of continuously passing large quantities of freshly-heated air through the sudatory chambers; exposing, however, the heating apparatus, so that a maximum of radiant heat may be obtained; and carefully guarding against injuring the air whilst raising its temperature. If only existing baths were in perfect harmony with this principle, one would have little cause for complaint, and might the more leisurely await the perfecting of the true radiating principle of heating, which I am satisfied is the one upon which we must base all our hopes for the future of the "Turkish" bath.

For practical purposes, it will suffice if the method of heating and ventilating a bath on the hot-air principle be explained. This I shall now do, and subsequently give plans and instructions for methods of heating and ventilating on systems where, by the exposure of the heating surfaces of furnaces, a large proportion of radiant heat is thrown into the hot-rooms.

The necessary appliances, and arrangements for the heating and ventilation of a bath on the ordinary hot-air [Pg 63] principle comprise a furnace in its chamber, with flues or shafts supplying cold, and drawing off the heated air, and a stokery with provisions for firing and storing coke, &c. Too often the stokery is unscrupulously cramped, and the life of the stoker thereby rendered anything but pleasant. Its design is a simple matter, and perhaps for this reason neglected. The arrangement and construction of the furnace chamber requires care, and the selection of a stove or furnace great judgment. As regards the latter feature, the most important point to consider is the nature of the heating or radiating surfaces. What will raise the air to the required temperature, without in the process depriving it in any way of its vitalising elements, and without adulterating it with either smoke and fumes from leakage, or with particles of foreign matter given off from the material employed in its construction?

There is nothing really better as a radiating surface than ordinary firebrick. From this material a soft heat is given off, differing in quality from that obtained from iron. An iron furnace, however, requires less thought in design, gives less trouble in fitting up, and is cheap, economical, and expeditious. Stoves, therefore, with an iron radiating surface, have been largely adopted in the past, in spite of the objection that, when super-heated, particles of metal are thrown into the air of the hot rooms. Of iron furnaces there are many placed before the public; but though all are doubtless suited to ordinary requirements, there are few that are capable of creditably fulfilling the conditions indispensable for the hygienic heating of the air of a Turkish bath. [Pg 64]

These conditions may be summarised as follows:—

1. A maximum of heating-surface, with a minimum of grate space.

2. Perfect immunity from the danger of leakage from the furnace into the hot-air chamber or conduit.

3. Freedom from the defect of liability to overheat the air.

4. Inability to adulterate the air by throwing off matter from the heating surfaces.

Such primary essentials must be constantly borne in mind by the designer of furnaces for the Turkish bath. Their importance must be obvious to all.

Of the many iron stoves, Messrs. Constantine's "Convoluted" stove has been adopted the most frequently, as an eminently practical furnace for the effective heating of the sudatory chambers. The appearance of this stove is familiar to all architects, and it will be unnecessary, in these pages, to minutely describe its construction.

The method of constructing a furnace suitable for a small public bath is, however, shown at Fig. 6. The excavations for stokery and heating chamber being completed, and the position of the furnace determined a solid foundation of concrete must be prepared, upon which the brickwork to support the stove must be laid. At the same time, the foundations for walls of furnace chamber, stokery, coke store, and the side walls for the horizontal cold-air conducting flues will be prepared. These latter must then be built in half-brick with glazed interior face, and the furnace inclosed in similar work, as shown in perspective sketch. The flues must be covered [Pg 65] with York stone slabs 3 in. thick, up to within three inches or so of the convolutions of the stove, at which distance the side walls of the furnace must be erected, the back one similarly, and the front one round the four projecting doors, which are, respectively, the ash-pit door, the fire door, and two doors for cleansing the horizontal smoke-box and interior of convolutions. The furnace walls must be continued up to a few inches above the bend of iron smoke flue, and then—if, as shown, the furnace be small—covered with a 4-in. York slab in one piece. If the furnace be large, a flat brick arch must form the [Pg 66] covering, as at Fig. 8, where this arch supports the flooring of the laconicum. The openings for the admission of the heated air into the conduit leading into the hot rooms may be either directly above, as shown in the last-named illustration, or in the side, as in Fig. 6, with inclined flues. As a rule, it is more economical, in heating on the principle now under consideration, to place the furnace below the level of the hot rooms; but if desirable to place both on one level, the back wall of the furnace chamber becomes the party wall of the laconicum, and it must be stopped short of the ceiling, and the air debouched over it.

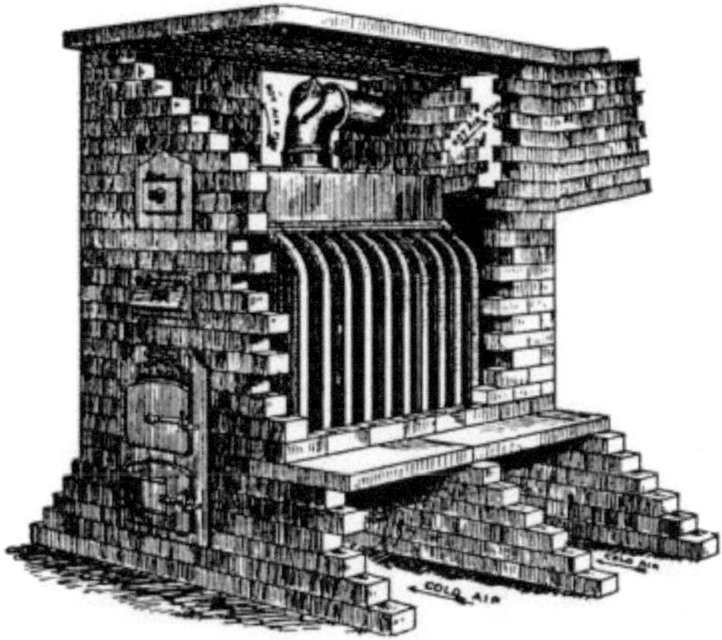

Fig. 6.
View of a small Furnace Chamber, with portion of wall broken away to show the "Convoluted" Stove.

In cheap baths the interior face of furnace chamber may be of stock brickwork; but best glazed work should be adopted in good ones. All hot and cold-air ducts should be similarly lined with glazed ware. In first-class work the floors of horizontal and inclined flues should be of white glazed tiles set in cement. Manholes must be provided for cleaning when necessary. Every portion of furnace chamber, flues, shafts, and conduits for hot and cold air must be "get-at-able" either by means of manholes or by long brushes. Air-tight doors must be indicated on the plans wherever this necessity demands them.

The iron smoke-pipe from furnace must be conducted to the smoke flue, and the connection between furnace chamber and flue hermetically sealed. The walls for a small furnace chamber need not be more than 4½ in. thick. Large furnaces require walls one-brick thick. [Pg 67]

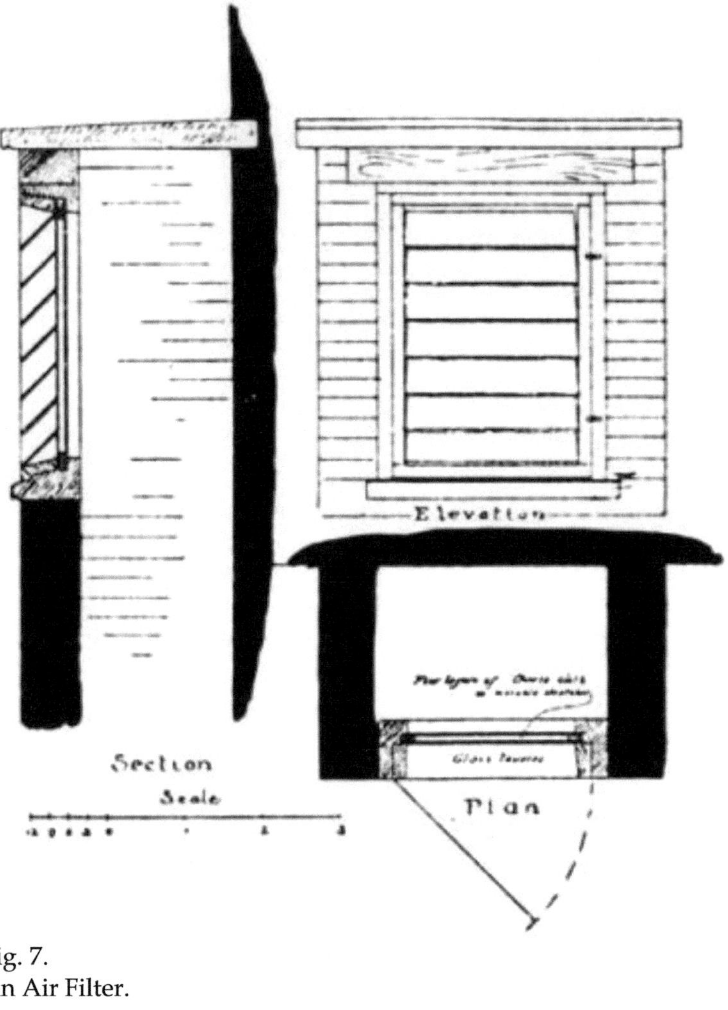

Fig. 7.
An Air Filter.

The cold-air flues leading from either side of the furnace must be conducted to their respective inlets. If possible, at least two inlets should be provided, facing different ways: this with regard to the possibility of certain winds drawing the air out where it is wanted to enter. The openings should be vertical, like windows, and, in cities, furnished with a solid frame and casement, fitted with louvres of plate glass with polished edges. Between the rebate and the casement it is a good plan to leave a space of an inch and a half for a movable stretcher-frame holding several layers of "cheese-cloth" to filter the air. The construction of such an air filter is shown at Fig. 7. The glass louvres keep out the wet, and throw off coarse particles of falling soot; and the provision of a movable stretcher permits the cloths to be frequently changed for clean ones—a very [Pg 68] important point, though little heeded, if not, perhaps, wholly ignored.

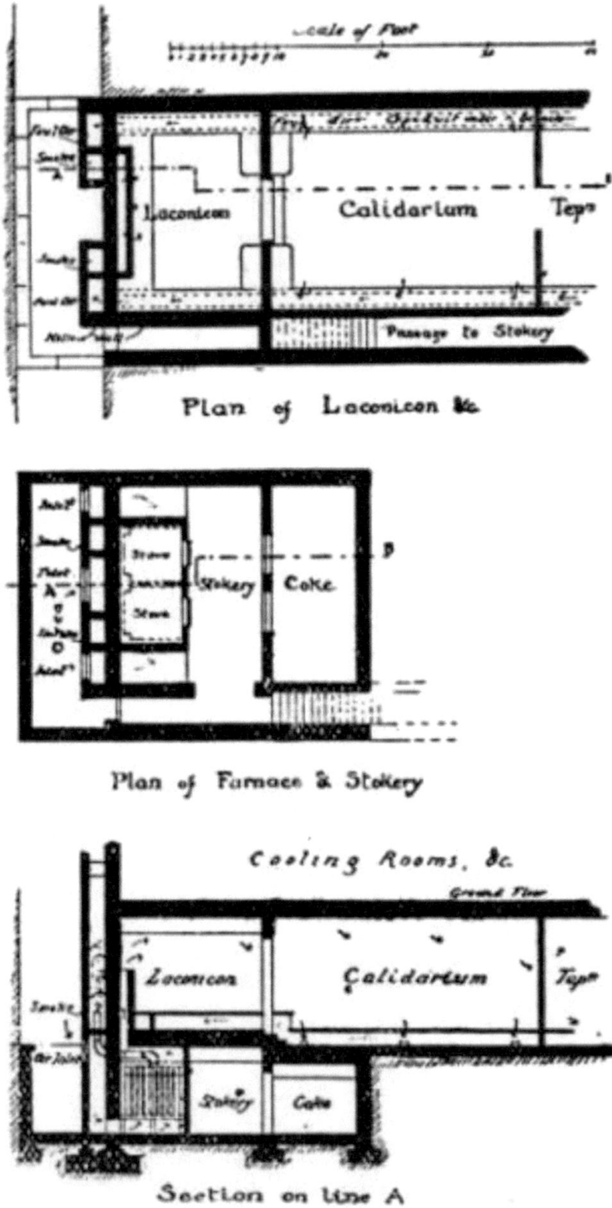
Laconicon
Calidarium
Tep^m
Passage to Stokery
Plan of Laconicon &c
Stokery
Coke
Plan of Furnace & Stokery
Cooling Rooms, &c.
Ground Floor
Laconicon
Calidarium
Tep^m
Stokery
Coke
Section on line A

Fig. 8.

Plans and Section of a Furnace Chamber, &c., for a Bath on the ordinary Hot-air Principle.
View larger image

The position of air intake is a matter of great importance, especially in large towns. It evidently is bad to draw a supply of air from the bottom of an area. Even the position shown in Fig. 8 is not good: the shaft [Pg 69] should be carried higher. The best places for the intakes are where there is always a current of pure air blowing, and away from smoky chimneys. Theoretically, it would seem that the higher the level of intake the better; but in cities, by going high we get among the belching chimney-tops, even if we escape the stagnation below. Moreover, a high inlet with a strong wind tending to exhaust the air in the shaft might find the architect with the cold air sweeping through his bath, and all the heated air rushing up the supply-shaft. A large "lobster-back" automatically turning *towards* the wind, would in many cases prevent such a disastrous result. Even in low-level intakes, as I have said, trouble will sometimes arise from the same cause. This may be remedied by providing more than one inlet, so that only the one facing the current of air will be employed, the other being closed, which could be effected by fixing the glass louvres, spoken of above, on pivots, and connecting them with a rod and adjustable rack. It would be a very simple matter to make the wind itself automatically open and shut the louvres.

The theory of the heating and ventilation of the hot rooms requires most careful study, and the particular scheme to be adopted in any new bath must be well considered with respect to the restrictions of the site. At Fig. 8, I have endeavoured to show how to make the best of what is perhaps a bad job: the site only admits of ventilation at a back area, it is impossible to construct flues anywhere else, and the fresh air must be drawn from the same area. On the ground floor are cooling and dressing rooms; the bath rooms are in the basement [Pg 70] and the furnace in a sub-basement, reached from a passage at the end of the stairs for the bather. Two convoluted stoves are shown in a vault; three air-inlets are provided, and the foul air is drawn up into the smoke flues, two in number, which, above, could join one another. Let us follow the air in its passage through the bath. Entering at the intakes, any coarse impurities are thrown off by the smooth louvres, and the tendency of finer particles to rush in is checked by the stretched canvas cheese-cloths. Thus deprived of its actually visible impurities, the air passes through a longer or shorter conduit of glazed brickwork until it reaches the horizontal flues running to beneath the furnace walls, along which it is rapidly drawn, and, ascending between the walls and heating surfaces and between the two adjacent heating surfaces, absorbs the radiating heat and enters the laconicum by way of the rectangular shaft constructed above the vault spanning the two stoves.

Questions of temperature I will omit for the present. The air, on passing through the laconicum, will be practically pure, as it is in such great bulk compared with the number of occupants of this highly-heated chamber, and it will not be absolutely necessary to provide ventilators. These should commence in the calidarium, and should, in the scheme of ventilation here considered, be so disposed that the nearer they are to the lavatorium and shampooing-room, the more frequent will they become. The object of this disposition of outlets for vitiated air is, that the cross currents thus created may not interfere with the main flow from the heating chamber to the lavatorium. [Pg 71] Were too many ventilators to be placed near the hotter end of the sudatorium, this stream would be diverted. Too much of the freshly-heated air would flow out at these points, and the onward movement of the air would be enfeebled. There would then be difficulty in maintaining the temperature in the tepidarium and lavatorium.

In passing onward through the various rooms, two changes are wrought in the air: it loses so much of the caloric with which it is charged for every foot it travels, and it becomes laden with the exhalations from the lungs of the bathers. A large proportion of carbonic acid is thrown into the air, and as the normal temperature of the human body remains, in a healthy person, at about 98° Fahr., and rises but a few points even when submitted to the action of heat, these exhalations, in addition to being heavier than air, are very much below the average temperature of a sudatory chamber. Consequently they fall, and must be extracted at the floor level.

The total area of the outlets for vitiated air should be about equal to the area of the narrowest part of the shaft that conducts the fresh, hot air from the heating chamber. Thus, supposing the latter to be 5 superficial feet, and the size of outlet ventilators a clear 12 in. by 3 in., there may be 20 ventilators disposed round the bath-rooms, say 4 in the calidarium, 7 in the tepidarium, and 9 in the combined shampooing room and lavatorium.

In the diagrams at Figs. 8 and 9 the foul air conduit is the space comprised under the marble-topped benches running round the hot rooms. At the end of the laco [Pg 72] nicum they enter flues, which I have shown as running side by side with the smoke flues.

Other methods of heating the air, besides those mentioned, include coils of iron flue-pipes in a brick chamber—a principle that has been frequently adopted in the past—and plain cylindrical iron radiating stoves, such as employed at the Hammam in Jermyn Street.

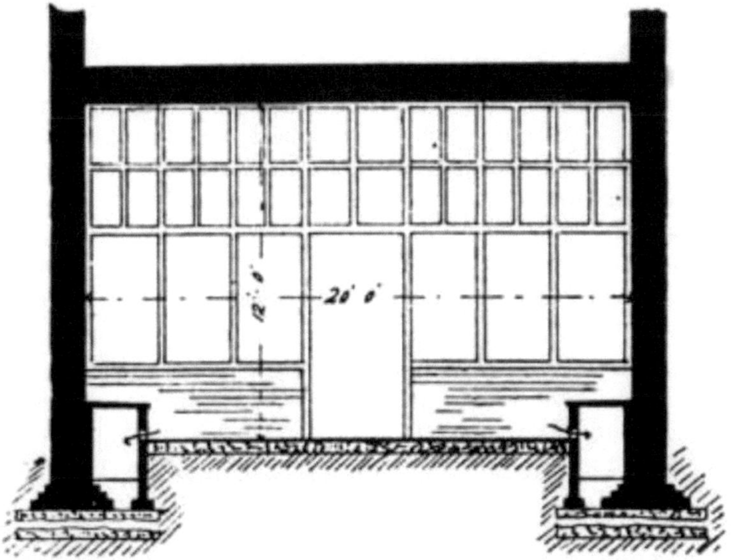

Fig. 9.
Section of Hot Room, showing Foul-air Conduit.

In the latter plan, however, a great expense is created by the large number of furnace-fires to be kept constantly burning. An exposed stove in a hot room, has, moreover, the objection to its use that it reheats the air in the bath, which should never on any account be done.

If the iron stove-pipe system is adopted, a furnace similar to the one shown at Fig. 10 must be provided, and after an additional few feet of brick flue the iron pipe would commence and turn back upon itself much as the flue in the fire-brick furnace. Proper supports must be [Pg 73] provided, and the pipes must be stout and jointed together with expansion joints, otherwise considerable difficulty will be found in keeping a long length of flue pipe perfectly free from leakage. Furnaces on this principle may be designed so that they throw a certain amount of radiant heat direct into the hot-rooms, and they possess this advantage over a mere stove, that they warm the air more gradually. The furnace should be built adjoining the laconicum, the partition wall being of 4½-inch glazed brick-work, having a large number of small openings made therein by leaving void spaces as described further on for the fireclay heating apparatus. Behind this wall the iron flue-pipe should be placed, turning back upon itself, as described above, for perhaps half-a-dozen times, and ending in the vertical brick flue. The furnace itself should be of fire-clay, and so designed that its utmost heating power may be economically employed in warming the incoming air, which should pass over the furnace and iron flues, through the holes in partition wall, and thus into the hot rooms. The flue, if of wrought iron, should be rectangular in section, but if of cast-iron it should be round.

The most economical way of obtaining a high temperature in a small, inexpensive, and unpretentious private bath is by means of a common laundry stove, with a longer or shorter length of iron flue in the apartment. This is the cheapest and quickest method of raising the temperature of a room for sudorific purposes. [Pg 74]

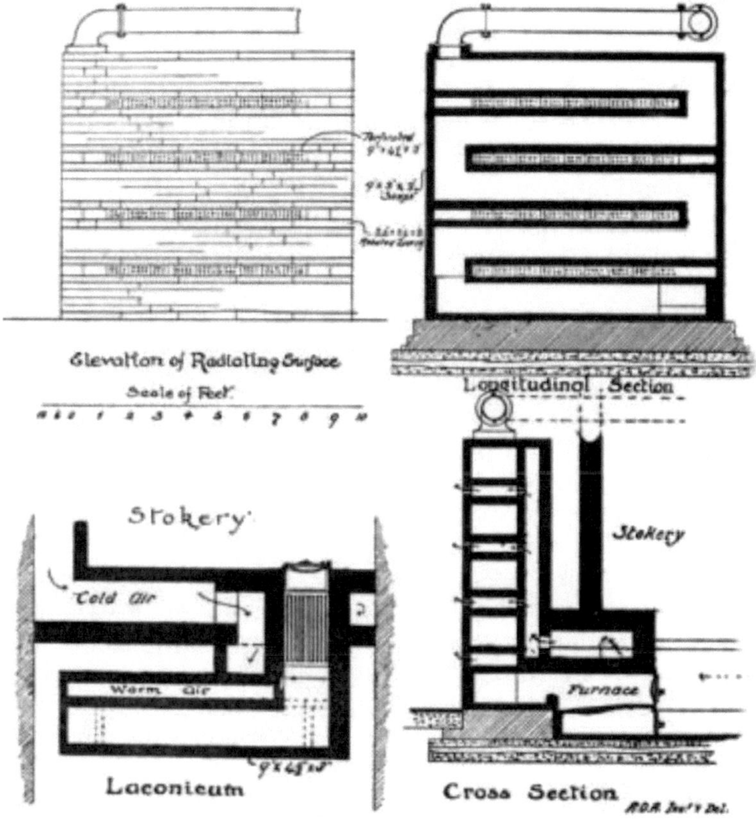

Fig. 10.
A Fireclay Heating Apparatus.
View larger image

To turn to methods of heating from a radiating surface of firebrick, at Fig. 10 I have given the plan, elevation, and sections of a fireclay heating apparatus. It is constructed wholly of fireclay—fireclay bricks, quarries, and cement. In the main it consists of a long flue of firebricks and slabs, which coils backwards and forwards over itself till the desired amount of radiating [Pg 75] surface is gained. Between the coils are spaces for super-heating the air already warmed by passing over the actual furnace and into the warm air chamber, the air passing through by means of perforated bricks. The illustration shows a simple furnace; but it would be an easy matter to improve upon this by providing iron air-tight doors lined with fireclay, for cleansing flues and air-chambers. The example given is only suited to heat a small public bath. For a large set of hot rooms, a compound apparatus could be constructed by placing an additional furnace in a sub-basement, the one on the level of the sudatory supplying radiant heat, and the lower one hot air. Two such apparatus might be placed one behind the other, end to end, or might form the *sides* of the laconicum; the last plan, however, being the least to be recommended, as in such positions they would not directly radiate their heat into the adjoining hot rooms.

The advantage of such a furnace as that shown is that it supplies radiant heat of a most exhilarating kind, besides a proportion of heated air, and from a fireclay surface, the employment of which renders it absolutely impossible to overheat the air, or to contaminate it by deleterious particles resulting from the decomposition of metal. Moreover, the stoking of this class of furnace requires less arduous attention than an iron stove. Its disadvantage is that, should the temperature of the bath be allowed to fall markedly, it requires some time for the extra heat to be made up again. Inasmuch, however, as fires at public baths must be kept banked up overnight, this is not a matter of importance. It is this [Pg 76] very slowness of increase in temperature that constitutes the safeguard against that overheated air, the presence of which we can, with practice, detect by the smell in so many baths. The difficulties involved in the construction of a furnace of this nature relate to the prevention of cracking and consequent escape of sulphurous fumes and carbon into the air. The very simplicity of the construction of the flues and air-chambers constitutes the chief danger, as the chances are that, unless the architect stands by and sees every joint made, the work will be done badly. Absolutely faultless workmanship must be employed throughout, and the fireclay materials must be literally of the very best and soundest description. Every single joint must be perfectly made with fireclay cement or paste. The fireclay bricks, &c., must be selected with regard to the amount of indestructible silica in the clay, consistent with hardness and toughness. Homogeneity of material must be obtained, having regard to expansion and contraction. The same material used for the bricks, &c., worked into a paste, must be employed for the joints.

The design for a furnace on the principle shown at Fig. 10 must be prepared with constant regard to expansion and contraction in heating and cooling. Should this warning be disregarded, fractures will result. It will be seen, upon reference to the plans, that the block of flues and air spaces is left quite free, to allow of any expansion, the connection with the smoke-shaft being by means of an iron flue-pipe, which, being provided in considerable length before passing through the party-wall of laconicum and stokery, by its flexible nature [Pg 77] permits any slight movement in a vertical direction. If an "expansion" joint were provided, there would be a sufficient length of iron pipe if it passed direct from the junction with the heating apparatus into the stokery. So much of the iron flue as is in the laconicum must be coated with asbestos or some composition, or the heating will not be wholly by firebrick. The junction of iron flue and heating apparatus is shown by a cast-iron cap sliding over a projecting rim of fireclay, moulded into the last quarry cover, similar to the way in which cast-iron mouthpieces are fitted to retorts.

This heating apparatus is shown visible in the laconicum, but if thought desirable it could be screened by a wall of glazed bricks—9 in. and miss 4½ in. The 4½ by 3 in. holes can be arranged in diamond patterns. This screen wall, however, cuts off a large quantity of radiant heat.

The first flue past the actual furnace—shown with ordinary dead-plate, raking fire-bars, ashpit, fire-door, and ashpit door for regulating draught—has walls 4½ in. thick; above, smaller bricks, 3 in. wide; but in a larger apparatus, 9 in. and 4½ in. respectively would be required. The quarries between flues and air spaces are 24 in. by 24 in. by 3 in., with rebated joints. Larger covers would be more liable to crack at any provocation.

In addition to heating by means of furnaces, steam-heating may be employed, if found, as in many cases it would be, convenient and economical. The chief disadvantage of this method of heating Turkish baths, is the constant danger, however slight, of bursting a [Pg 78] pipe in the heating coil, which, by immediately filling the highly-heated atmosphere with vapour, might prove most disastrous to the occupants of the hot rooms, who would be seriously scalded. Nevertheless, the principle has been largely employed in the heating of the most recent Turkish baths in Germany.

If adopted it may be either on the hot-air or radiating plan, as in heating by means of furnaces. In the first method the fresh air is introduced into a chamber containing a coil of steam-pipes, and passes thence into the laconicum by a shaft or conduit, as in the case of air heated by a stove. In the second method, steam radiators—compact batteries of pipes—must be placed in recesses in the hot rooms, fresh air being introduced over them. The steam-pipes employed should be of the "small bore" type, about 5/8 inch internal diameter, and of wrought iron or copper. In order to ensure as far as possible against the danger of explosion, the system of pipes should be tested, when fixed, by severe hydraulic pressure.

It is certainly a great advantage, in point of ease and economy, to be able to warm a building, drive machinery, and heat Turkish and Russian baths from one boiler, which can readily be done, very ordinary pressures of steam giving sufficient heat to keep the radiators of the requisite temperature. But the nature of the heating accomplished by means of steam-pipes is very inferior to that from large radiating surfaces of firebrick.

The average temperatures of a public bath should range from about 110° in the shampooing rooms to [Pg 79] 250°-260° in the hottest part of the laconicum, taking the readings of the thermometer at a level of 6 ft. 6 in. above floor-line. Between the entrance of the heated air and its point of furthest travel in the shampooing rooms, the bather should be able to select any temperature that may be most agreeable to him, and as many find by experience that a certain degree of heat is best suited to themselves, it shows attention to the *habitués* of the bath, if the hot rooms are carefully maintained at the same uniform temperatures throughout the year. This may be 110°-120° in the shampooing rooms, 140° in the tepidarium, 180° in the calidarium, and 250° in the laconicum. These must be the maxima of the average temperatures of each room at 6 ft. 6 in. above the floor. In a pure atmosphere the highest temperatures are comfortable, but in a foul one they become insupportable.

In a good bath, where there is a rapid and continuous flow of air, there will be comparatively little difference between the temperature at say 4 ft., 6 ft., and 8 ft. above the floor. In badly-ventilated rooms, where the air stagnates, there will be a considerable difference. And here we may note a serious objection to the heating of a bath by convection; for while the head may be in a high degree of heat the feet are in comparatively cool air, whereas, if possible, it should be just the reverse. In convected heat, this of course applies in its entirety, as where so-called radiant heat is employed the evil is not quite so marked. And here, too, we may note the admirable nature of the Roman system of heating, where the floors radiated the majority of the heat, and [Pg 80] the walls a slightly less amount. The fresh air under the ancient system must have entered through the cooler rooms, and being drawn towards the *calidarium* found its exit through the ceilings, at times by way of the regulating device mentioned by Vitruvius. Thus the ancient bather would not suffer the inconvenience that accrues to the bather in the modern hot-air bath, whose head, when he is standing upright, is in a considerably higher temperature than any other portion of his body.

The temperature of a bath should not be regulated by the firing of the furnace. This should be regularly stoked, and kept at one uniform heat-giving condition. Bad firing and forced firing may crack the stove should it be of iron, and the air may be overheated. The temperature should be regulated by means of the hit-and-miss ventilators at the floor level. Fanlights between the various hot rooms, with screw-rod adjustment, serve as a means for regulating their relative temperatures.

The heating power of furnaces must be studied. Having calculated the cubical contents of the rooms to be heated, and given the heating power of the stove or apparatus to be employed per cwt. of metal or superficial foot of radiating surface, we arrive at the necessary size.

Messrs. Constantine give the following tables to show the heating power of the "Convoluted" stove. The figures give the requisite size of stove to raise the air to about the relative temperatures I have mentioned before, and with ordinary firing. [Pg 81]

Weight of metal.	Sq. ft. of heating surface.	Area capable of heating.

cwt.	sq. ft.	cub. ft.
14	35	500
20	55	1,200
22	69	2,000
34	119	3,500
36	139	5,000
45	180	8,000
50	231	12,000
56	296	16,000

When different kinds of heating apparatus are employed, their heating power must be carefully ascertained and calculations entered into, or it may be found necessary to resort to the costly and humiliating process of dragging out the stove or pulling down the furnace and refitting a larger one. This point is worth attention. Such mistakes are not unfrequently made.

As regards the amount of air that should flow through the hot rooms, an allowance of 40 cubic feet per head per minute should be the minimum, if purity of atmosphere is to be maintained. In a bath, the importance of perfect ventilation cannot possibly be over estimated, as not only has the respired air from the lungs to be removed, but also the deleterious exhalations from the skin which are produced by perspiration.

The allowance of 40 cubic feet per head per minute should not, if properly distributed, cause an unpleasant draught in any part of the hot rooms; for it must be remembered that even in a highly-heated atmosphere a waft of air of the same temperature is felt to be cold. The main thing to be studied in this provision of a large volume of air is that the cold inlet be ample, and the [Pg 82] passage from this intake to the point where the air is debouched into the laconicum equally roomy and unobstructed. The rapidity of flow will depend upon the means provided for the extraction of the foul air. With large horizontal flues, and a capacious and tall shaft, the so-called natural system of ventilation will be as effective as could be desired. Greater extraction power is gained if in the brick stack a smoke-pipe can be placed running up the whole height. In many cases mechanical ventilation could be employed with the greatest benefit. A powerful air-propeller fixed at the end of a system of horizontal flues under the floors of the hot rooms, and running so as to exhaust, would do away with all the objectionable odours and nastiness of many baths.

The purity or foulness of the air in the hot rooms forms all the difference between a good bath and a bad one, which latter is infinitely worse than no bath at all. There exist, at the present time, scores of baths where the odours of the sudatory chambers are nauseating. Such foulness arises from stagnation of the air. There is no continuous flow, and the respirations and exhalations of the bathers are not removed. A system of ventilation may be pointed out, but it is on the wrong principle, and does not act. There is no change of air. The atmosphere of such places becomes pestilential.

Owing to the expansion by heat, a relatively greater volume of air enters the laconicum than the cold intake. This fact, however, does not practically affect the arrangements for ventilation, &c. Theoretically, how [Pg 83] ever, it would seem to demand that the shaft conducting from furnace to hot rooms should be of greater sectional area than that to the furnace from the intake—about one-third larger—and that the total area of outlets for the escape of vitiated air should be about midway between the two.

The whole principle of the ventilation of the hot rooms of a Turkish bath resolves itself, primarily, into the fact that we have to continually remove *the bottom layer of air.* The provision of the foul-air conduits below the floor level is equivalent to providing a suspended floor with a hollow space under. This is just the reverse of the principle of ventilating rooms of ordinary temperature, where we require to constantly remove the top layer, and often actually do so when we provide false ceilings to passages, &c.

The ventilators placed at the floor level of the hot rooms should be actually so, and not 3 in. or 6 in. above. Long, wide gratings 6 in. deep are preferable to those of deeper and narrower design. In theory, indeed, the whole circumference of the hot rooms should be lined round with gratings, thus making the sudatorium like a lidless box inverted, into which hot air is thrown and escapes all round the bottom edges.

There is one point about the circulation of air in a set of hot rooms that requires considerable attention, and that is the *back-flow* along the floor. In any bath where hot air is supplied, if the bather will hold his linen "check" across the top of the doorway between the rooms he will find that the air is flowing from the laconicum to the shampooing room. If, however, the sheet [Pg 84] be held across the lower portion of the doorway, he will find that there is a current of air setting in an opposite direction—from the shampooing room to the laconicum. This is shown at Fig. 11.

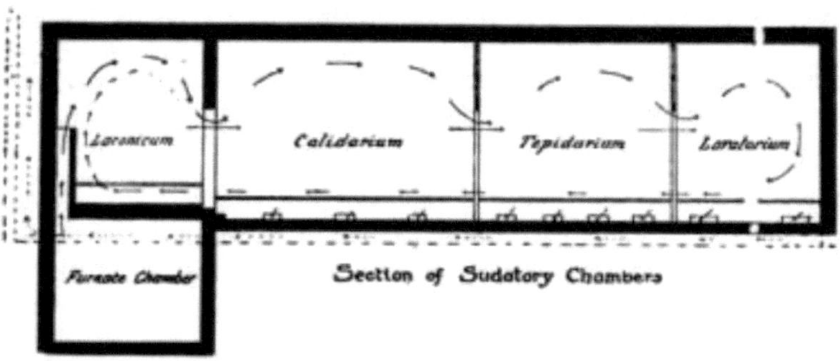

Fig. 11.
Longitudinal Section of Sudatory Chambers.
View larger image

It will be seen from the diagram that the bather is really in this back-flow when he is standing between and [Pg 85] in a line with the doors of the hot rooms. All the air appears to be travelling along the top of the bath, and the bather reclining on the marble-topped benches would seem to be bathed in air that has passed along the top of the bath, round the shampooing rooms, and back along the floor. In reality, however, it is only from door to door that the currents exist exactly as shown at the diagram, Fig. 11, there being a secondary circulating process in each room.

This circulation of air will exist in any bath heated on the modern system—that is to say, where freshly-heated air is passed in in sufficient quantity. It is a natural result, and tends to distribute the heat more equally. The back-flow is only objectionable when a door is opened direct from the heated shampooing rooms to a cooler apartment, as the plunge bath chamber. The bather standing in a line between the doorways may then feel a cold draught. To guard against this, double doors, with a small lobby between, should be provided to any means of communication with a cold chamber.

A set of hot rooms could be constructed so that the bather would be in the top current of air that flows from the heating apparatus. By reference to Fig. 11 the reader will understand that by the provision of a platform or grating midway between the floor and ceiling this end would be attained.

The atmosphere of the sudatorium must be perfectly free from vapour. "Perfect dryness of the air," says Mr. Urquhart, "is indispensable to the enduring of a high temperature.... This dryness is further requisite for electrical isolation. With vapour in the chamber an [Pg 86] atmosphere is created injurious to health and conducive to disease. It is the very condition in which low, putrid, and typhus fevers flourish. The electrical spark will not ignite in such an atmosphere, and the magnet will lose its attractive power. We all know the difference of our own sensations on a dry and on a damp day." [Pg 87]

CHAPTER VI.

WATER FITTINGS AND APPLIANCES.

The water-fittings of a Turkish bath include a boiler of some form for heating the water, a cold-water cistern, and a hot-water tank; supply-pipes, flow and return pipes, and branch pipes; lavatorium fittings, comprising bowls, basins, and cocks; douche room fittings, as the "needle" bath, shower, douche, spray, and "wave" baths; a warm shower-bath for bathers entering the bath, or desiring such a shower at intervals; and the fittings of the plunge bath. In addition to this there may be required a drinking fountain in the tepidarium, and an ornamental fountain in the frigidarium; lavatories in various positions; and, possibly, fittings and appliances for the laundry.

Premising an ample supply of pure water, it must be brought into the building through a water-meter to the cold water cistern, which should be at a sufficiently high level to obtain a good "head." This cistern must be capacious and properly connected, on the ordinary circulating principle, with a hot water tank and boiler. Of suitable boilers there are several in the market, of many and varied designs. Simplicity of construction should be the guide to a selection. The boiler will perhaps its most conveniently placed in the stokery, and have be [Pg 88] separate furnace and flue, any scheme for combining the heating of the hot rooms and of the water being out of the question. In small baths, however, the hot-water tank may, for economy's sake, be placed near the ceiling in the laconicum. Where waste steam can be obtained, a water super-heater, with steam coil, may be employed with advantage; but in the majority of cases the ordinary circulating system will be found the most suitable.

The supply-pipes must be of large section, and indeed, the whole scheme of water-fitting should be liberal. It must be remembered that, in addition to the wants of the lavatorium and douche room, plunge, &c., there will be a large amount of water required for laundry purposes, if washing be done upon the premises.

The cold supply cistern may, by the exigencies of the case, be kept down as low as the ceiling of the bath-rooms, and be placed over some subsidiary apartment. This does not give much pressure of water. For all purposes it is best to have the cistern at a minimum height of about 20 ft. above the draw-off taps and valves of the various bathing appliances. This will ensure a good head of water, and make the douche a formidable affair.

The pipes, unions, tees, valves, and cocks should all be of the best description in so important a work as the fitting-up of a public bath. Ordinary bungling plumbing is here out of place. Lead piping should be discarded for all but very cheap work, and iron employed in its stead, with proper screwed joints, angles, and tees. [Pg 89] Should there be sufficient means, *copper* piping should be employed for anything under 1 in. internal diameter, and gunmetal should be used for unions, &c., and for cocks and valves.

Handsome, large, and well-made water-fittings conduce, in no small degree, to the effect of a bath. There should be no attempt at hiding away of pipes, &c. They should be made features of the bath, and be designed with care and neatly finished. Every pipe, joint, and connection should be prearranged, and the means of fixing and supporting the same carefully designed. Boxings, and the like, should be discarded, and everything frankly exhibited. The day for mysterious plumbing has gone by. There is some beauty even in a pipe.

To consider the fittings, we will commence with the lavatorium. Branches from the hot and cold water supply pipes must be conducted to each shampooer's basin. These may be finished separately, with independent nozzles, as at Fig. 12; or the pipes may be connected with the valve shown at Fig. 13, about 18 in. above the basin, the outlet of the valve being fitted with a foot or 15 in. of indiarubber hose. In the latter case the pipes and valve would stand some 9 in. from the wall, and depend from the horizontal supply pipes, which in their turn could be carried on wrought-iron brackets affixed to the wall, or be hung by iron ties, as indicated by dotted lines at Fig. 16. The *internal* diameter—the measurement given in all the figures—of these branch pipes to taps over shampooing basins should be 3/4 in. [Pg 90]

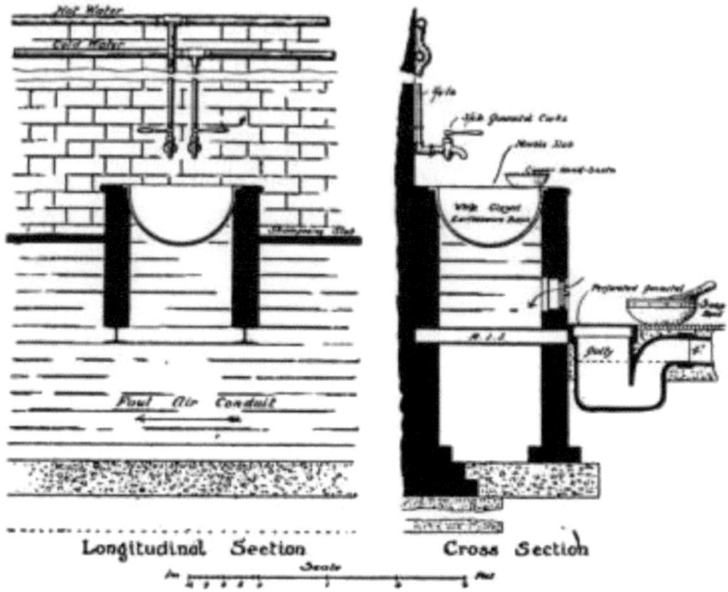

Fig. 12.
A Shampooing Basin.

Cocks and valves for the purposes of the Turkish bath are best of the "gland" pattern. They should have bold handles. Those of the screw-down type are useless, except as stop-cocks. Roundways should be used, and, to insure freedom of running, the turning part should be equal to the inner diameter of the pipes. The whole should be of gunmetal, and, if the pipes to [Pg 91] be used be of iron, screwed at the end. Fig. 13 shows the type of valve to be employed to regulate the temperature of water for shower baths, &c. To be useful, as well as bold and effective in appearance, the handles should be large.

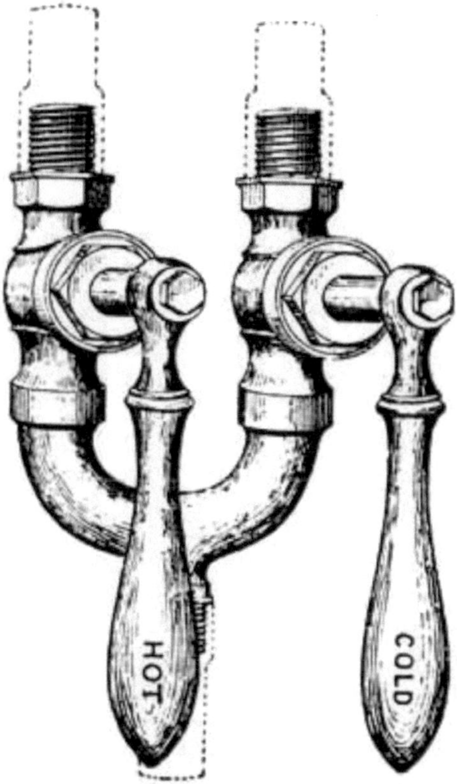

Fig. 13.
Valve for Regulating Temperature of Water.

In every case, the cold water must be placed on the right hand, and the hot on the left.

The earthenware basin is provided to hold water [Pg 92] mixed to the required temperature. A waste and overflow are not shown in the illustration, but they should be provided. The basin is best wide and shallow—shallower than shown. There should be no overhanging ledge to catch the shampooer's hand-basin; for this reason I have shown, at Fig. 12, the basin sunk into the marble slab, instead of the marble being on top, as ordinary. The copper hand-basin is provided for the shampooer to take water from the earthenware basin and throw over the shampooing slab, or over the bather. In addition, a wooden, copper-banded soap-bowl must be provided.

Should there be a row of shampooing basins and benches, the horizontal supply-pipes must be continued along the wall, and branches dropped to each basin. The basins are most conveniently placed when raised somewhat higher than the benches. In the illustration given, I have shown how to arrange horizontal foul-air flues under the basins. In other cases the fixing of the basins will be much simpler. For pure lavatorium purposes these basins, cocks, &c., are all the water-fittings to be considered; but in an apartment combining the purposes of douche room—and perhaps a plunge bath chamber—as well as a washing and massage room, more or less of the fittings about to be described will have to be accommodated.

The tonic appliances for treating the bather subsequently to the shampooing, the soaping, and the cleansing, are various. The most useful is the simple shower bath, with a very large rose, and amply supplied with water through a regulating valve. It is employed for [Pg 93] thoroughly cleansing the bather before he enters the plunge, whose waters are for the common use of all. In many small baths its place is efficiently taken by an ordinary hand rose or spray of the kind shown at Fig. 15. The shower proper is usually fixed above the "needle" bath, as at Fig. 14, or formed by a continuation of the "backbone" of the needle. It is best to have separate regulating valves for the needle and shower, as at Fig. 16; but at Fig. 14 it is shown with a branch from the pipe conducting to the needle, and with stop cocks. The needle-bath is a skeleton-like structure having a large hollow backbone and branching ribs. The water ascends the backbone, and, passing into the ribs, squirts out of small holes punctured in their internal circumferences. The bather stands in the centre of the apparatus, with the ribs encircling him. The ribs should be of 1/2-in. copper piping, the backbone and lesser supports being of iron, 2½ and 1½ in. diameter respectively. In a convenient position for the attendant must be placed the regulating valve.

A more elaborate contrivance may be made, which will include needle, shower, ascending shower, spinal douche, and back shower; but this should be left for hydropathic institutions and invalids. Simplicity in these matters should be the great desideratum. The above-named additions, however, may be briefly described. At Fig. 14 I have indicated the position of ascending shower. It would be connected with the pipe supplying needle and shower, and have a stop-cock. The spinal douche is a little nozzle behind the shower proper, and should have similar connection with the [Pg 94] supply-pipe. The back shower or spinal spray would be a rose placed about half-way up the iron backbone, and be connected in the same manner. Avoid these complications in a bath for healthy persons.

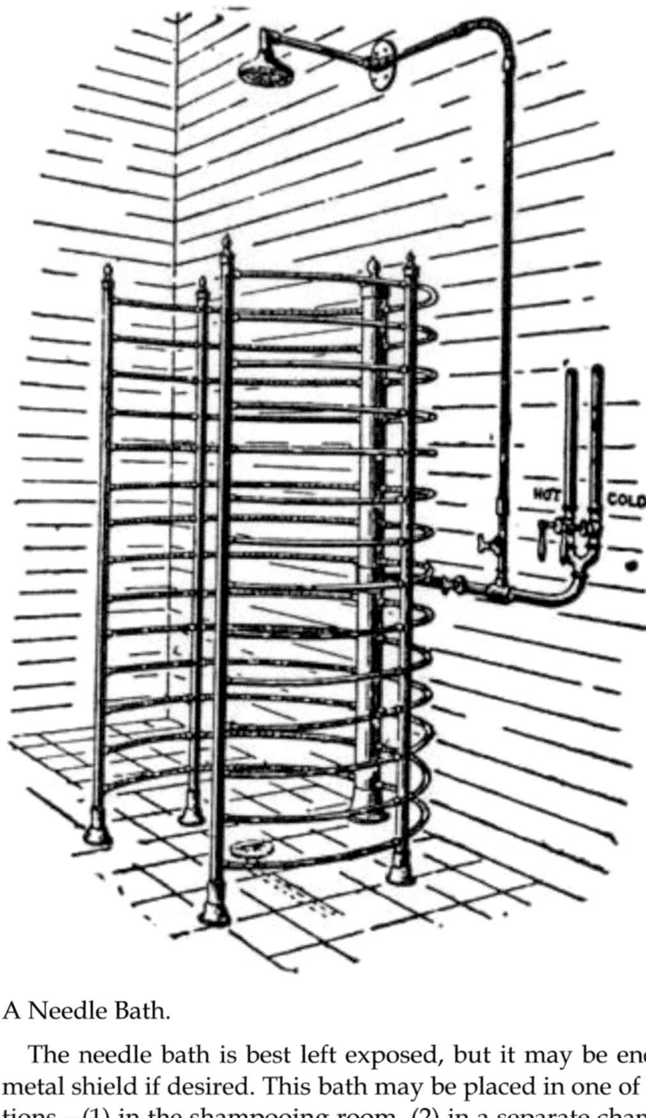

Fig. 14.

A Needle Bath.

The needle bath is best left exposed, but it may be enclosed in a metal shield if desired. This bath may be placed in one of three positions—(1) in the shampooing room, (2) in a separate chamber, (3) in the plunge bath chamber. It is most conveniently placed where the bather passes it *en route* from the washing room to the [Pg 95] plunge. For this appliance a good head of water is absolutely essential, as with a low pressure it is very ineffective. The illustration shows the bath standing on iron shoes. If fixed in a corner, as ordinarily, it can be secured to the wall by such cramps or brackets as may be necessary.

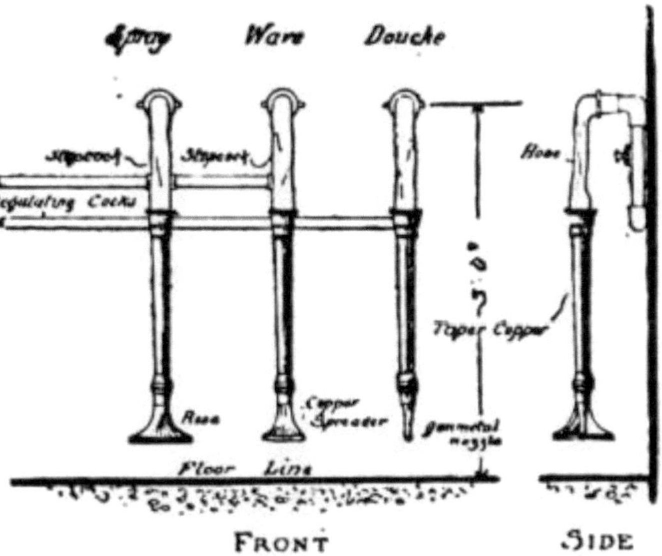

Fig. 15.
Spray, Wave, and Douche Baths.

Besides the needle and shower, as above, the tonic bathing appliances may include an ordinary horizontal douche that can be pointed in any direction, a spray, or large rose, and a "wave." These three appliances may be placed together as at Fig. 15. They are connected to the pipes from the regulating valves by means of a foot or so of flexible hose. To this is secured a tapering copper pipe. The douche has a gunmetal nozzle. It is directed against the back and spine, but must not be used upon the head or chest. With a good head of water this is a most powerful appliance, feeling more like a rod of some solid substance pressing against one than a stream of water. The "wave" [Pg 96] is formed by a copper spreader. The spray is simply a large rose, 6 in. or 8 in. diameter.

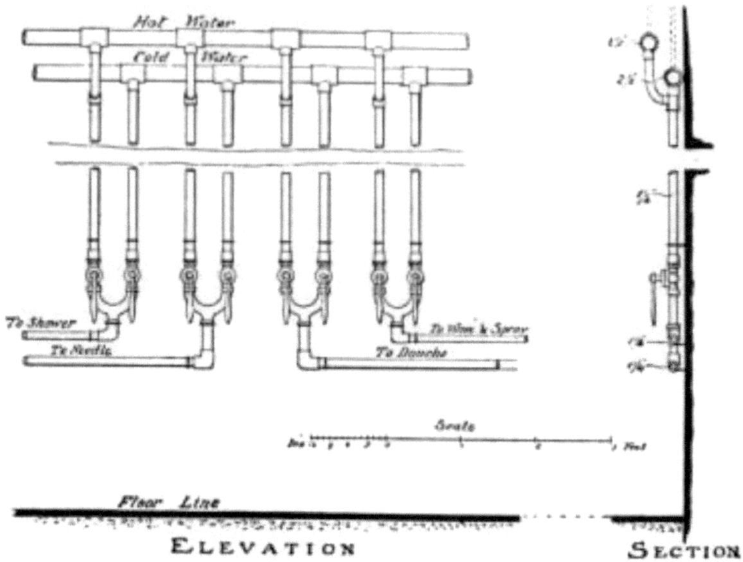

Fig. 16.
Regulating Valves for Needle, Douche, &c.

It may be found convenient to arrange the valves for the whole of the above-mentioned appliances together, as at Fig. 16. Each pair of hot and cold handles are here brought together. These handles should be long, so as to admit of easy regulating of the tempera [Pg 97] ture of the water; they may well be 9 in. in length. The douche, wave, and spray should be kept as close as possible to the handles that regulate their temperature.

I would repeat the caution that it is very necessary to beware of complications in these water-fittings and appliances. Some of the more "fussy" contrivances—as, for example, the elaborated needle bath as above described—require so much regulating, and so many valves and stop-cocks, that it is quite an undertaking for the attendant to set them going. Simplicity in design and construction should be observed in this work: the pipes as few as need be; the valves as simple as possible; and the whole put together in a manner that will permit of their being easily examined and repaired.

I have before hinted at the desirability of making some sort of provision whereby the bather may, on entering the bath, have a warm spray or shower, of any temperature that may be agreeable to him. In high class baths this feature should always be provided, as it is a great luxury, and, moreover, to certain constitutions a necessity, thus to be able to take such a shower before entering the hot rooms, or at such intervals during the sojourn in these apartments as may be desired. The proper position for this shower-bath requires some consideration. Were it only for the entering bather that it should be provided, it would be best placed in a lobby near the entrance to the hot rooms; but as the occupants of the hot rooms may frequently desire some such shower, it must be arranged with regard to this fact. It should be convenient for the entering bathers and for those in the [Pg 98] bath. A small chamber entered by doors from the lobby to the tepidarium, and also from the tepidarium itself, would be convenient. At times it may be placed in a nook off the shampooing room. Wherever it be placed, the apparatus provided for the purpose of the shower must be such as can be managed by the bather himself, so as not to take up the time of the attendants; and for this reason it must be capable of easy regulation, and free from liability of scalding the user, unless through gross carelessness. A valve with one handle only must be employed, as, unless the bather has had some practice, it is difficult to obtain this immunity from danger of scalding when two handles are used. A valve such as that shown at Fig. 17 should be employed. This valve must be so designed as to supply cold, tepid, and hot water *in regular gradation*—not intermittently, as do some valves of this description. It must be so placed that any one taking the shower may, whilst beneath the rose, be able to easily reach the handle. The rose should not be less than 6 in. or 7 in. diameter. Fig. 12 illustrates the complete fitting up of this bather's shower-bath.

In hydropathic establishments it might be an improvement to add a small foot-bath, formed by a sinking of about 6 in. in the floor, and filled with hot water; for physiologists tell us it is bad for invalids to enter the hot rooms with cold feet. Supply pipes, a waste, and overflow would have to be provided for this bath, and a marble seat might be placed round it. A marble coping and mosaic flooring would render it pleasing in appearance. [Pg 99]

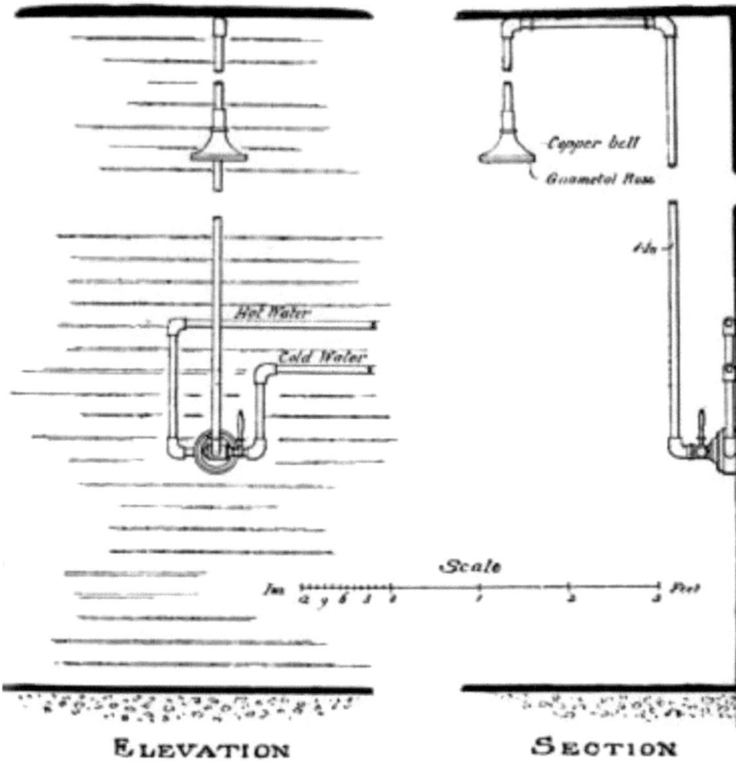

Fig. 17.
Bather's Shower Bath.

I have hereinbefore, at Fig. 4, given plan and sections of a plunge bath, and shown its water-fittings. The overflow and waste run into cast-iron drainpipes, which should be employed till outside the building. On the [Pg 100] end of the overflow pipe is screwed a gunmetal rose with leather packing, the screw-holes being drilled into the flange of pipe. For the waste I have shown a "disc" valve of gunmetal. This is similarly screwed to flange of pipe, and with leather packing. The valve is opened and closed by a movable rod. If *fixed*, it might catch the toes of the swimmer, and for this reason it would perhaps be best to set the valve itself back in a recess. Instead of this valve, an ordinary 4-in., 5-in., or 6-in. "plug" waste could be employed, but it is rather clumsy on such a scale. When practicable, a screw-down valve, with wheel and spindle outside the bath, is the best means of letting out the waste water. The supply-pipe should be connected with the main supply just after the water meter. The valve should be of the "screw-down" pattern, either with a thumb-screw, wheel and spindle, or a key.

In coast towns, where a *sea-water* plunge may be employed, a little rose on a bracket should be provided in a convenient position, for cleansing the hair from salt water.

Of the lavatory fittings in the cooling room, and of the "sanitary" water-fittings, it is unnecessary to speak, except to say that, in a place devoted to the attainment of cleanliness, plumbing of this nature should be as perfect as possible.

A drinking fountain is a desirable feature in the tepidarium of a bath of any pretension. It should be placed at the coolest end of the room, affixed to a wall, and provided with a supply-pipe, waste, [Pg 101] and tap of some sort. The bowl is best formed of glazed earthenware.

If an ornamental fountain be required in the frigidarium, it should be of terra-cotta or modelled glazed ware, and must be provided with supply-pipe, waste, and means of regulating the jet of water. A fountain is a very desirable addition to a cooling room, as it is restful to the ear, and may be made pleasant to the eye by means of flowers and plants arranged around and upon it. [Pg 102]

CHAPTER VII.

LIGHTING, DECORATING, AND FURNISHING.

Light and shade being the soul of all ornamental effect, we may well consider first the methods of lighting the bath. As a rule, much artificial light will be required. The hot rooms, being often in a basement, are as a rule but feebly illumined from areas and the like. Seeing that purity of atmosphere in these apartments is of so vital importance, the method of artificial lighting adopted should not be such as impregnates the air with obnoxious and harmful, if unnoticeable, fumes. Gas, for this reason, used in the ordinary manner, is objectionable, as the ventilation being by means of low-level exits for the foul air, the products of combustion must of necessity pass by and envelop persons below the burners, though, of course, in a diluted state. Should, therefore, gas-lighting be employed in a sudatory chamber, it should for preference be on one of those systems whereby the burner is cut off from the atmosphere of the room, and provision made for carrying off the fumes. Happily, the use of electric lighting is at last increasing with marked rapidity; and the incandescent light is admirably adapted for all purposes of the Turkish bath. Where it can possibly be adopted it is a great addition to a bath. [Pg 103]

For cooling room purposes gas is not so objectionable, except that it is heating, and assists in vitiating the atmosphere. But inasmuch as the fumes in this case will ascend with the general body of air, the objection to gas is much lessened in these apartments. Nevertheless, the electric light is the illuminant to be coveted.

The quality of the lighting in the cooling room should be toned and softened. It is not a place for brilliant general illumination, but rather for a soft light pervading the whole, and auxiliary lights where required, such as near couches, &c.—a system, in fact, diametrically opposed to sun-burner illumination. Nothing more objectionable of its kind can well be imagined than a glaring light in the ceiling of a cooling room. It would be found intolerable.

For practical purposes, the greatest amount of light required in any part of a frigidarium is that at the heads of the couches, where it must be of such strength as will admit of comfortable reading. One gas-burner, or one small incandescent lamp, to every two couches is a fair allowance. If effect be desired, there is, of course, much in the distribution of the illuminating agent that affects for good or evil, and the placing and the relative powers of the lamps or burners must be considered. The dominant point of light might be a prettily-designed lantern with a few brilliant points of colour in it, depending from a chain over a fountain, throwing its rays downwards on to the falling waters, and *not* in the eyes of those bathers who may be reclining upon the couches. [Pg 104]

Throughout the bath, in either natural or artificial lighting, by windows or lamps, it should be the aim not to throw strong light in the eyes of the bather—a principle of universal application, but especially to be regarded in a place where, more often than not, the occupants of the various apartments are reclining, *face upwards*, on benches or couches. In the hot rooms, as in the cooling room, little general illumination is required. A bright artificial light in such places seems especially painful to the eyes. What light, therefore, may be provided in the sudatory chambers, should be as diffused as possible, the additional lights for the few who practise reading in these apartments being so arranged as not to be objectionable to the majority of bathers. The lights should be shaded so as to throw their rays downwards in a very small compass.

Considerably more light is required in the lavatoria and shampooing rooms. In scheming the plan of bath rooms in a basement, where daylight can only be obtained at one point, it is desirable, if practicable, to arrange the shampooing room so that it may enjoy the benefit of this light.

For effect, the scale of lighting in the bath rooms may be a rather dark laconicum, and a gradually-increased amount of light from thence to the shampooing room. The plunge-bath chamber should be well lighted, but not above the tone of the frigidarium, or the bather will feel to be going from cheerfulness to comparative gloom, which would be unpleasant. A bright, warm light should be that in the plunge-bath chamber, with perhaps an ornamental lamp over the [Pg 105] bath itself; and if the intermediary staircase—should there be such a feature—be lighted on a lower scale, the effect on entering the frigidarium will be a cheerful one.

Decorating.

Under this heading, I would speak of the means of obtaining effect in a bath, of the materials to be employed, and of the design of features—of the effect of the whole and the proportions of its parts, rather than of anything implying the *laying on* of so-called ornament.

The architecture of a bath is *interior architecture* as distinct from that involving external work. Much of this, moreover, can often only be seen by artificial light. These two restrictions point to the employment, for the most part, of surface decoration, rather than of modelling—of tiles, mosaics, marbles, in place of mouldings, cornices, and pilasters.

There are three features of the bath that are fit subjects for handsome designing, and they are the frigidarium, the tepidarium, and the plunge bath. There is an excuse for elaborating the first two, in that these are the apartments in which the bather remains the longest time; and as for the plunge, it is in itself an object capable of giving a very pleasing effect. Over-elaboration—in respect to added ornament—in the hot rooms, however, gives an air of incongruity. Simplicity, with good proportions, seems here the most pleasing. The general effect of the hot rooms should be light, a [Pg 106] statement which is wholly in harmony with what I have said on their lighting, though it may not at first sight appear to be so. The tone of the ceilings and walls and floors should be light, the darkest portions being a dado. A generally dark and heavy tone of colouring is very oppressive in a sudatory chamber. Keep them light: light ceilings of plaster for cheap baths, and of lightly decorated, large, thin tiles, or lightly-tinted enamelled iron, for more expensive establishments; light walls of white, ivory, cream, or buff glazed bricks, without startling bands of a vulgar, as distinct from a really bold, contrast; and mosaic floors of a light filling-in and not too dark pattern. The risers to marble-topped benches may be of another tone, but not too dark; and, in place of a dado of bare glazed bricks, it is perhaps best to stretch Indian matting to keep the bather from the burning wall, as at Fig. 20. This will necessitate fillets affixed to plugs in the brickwork. Woodwork looks best dark and polished, affording an agreeable contrast to the lighter materials.

Bright points of colour may be obtained by stained glass in ceiling-lights or windows, and at night by coloured glass shades over lamps, &c.

The use of iron joists with glazed brick arches between is not to be recommended for the ceilings of the hot rooms. To say the least, it is a heavy-looking arrangement. Enamelled iron may be made to look very well if affixed in sheets of delicate tint with light patterns, and affixed with "buttons" with enamelled heads to the fireproof floors, as at Fig. 18. Large thin tiles make an admirable ceiling for small baths. They [Pg 107] may be fixed with ornamental wood fillets, or made with screw-holes and affixed to ceiling joists.

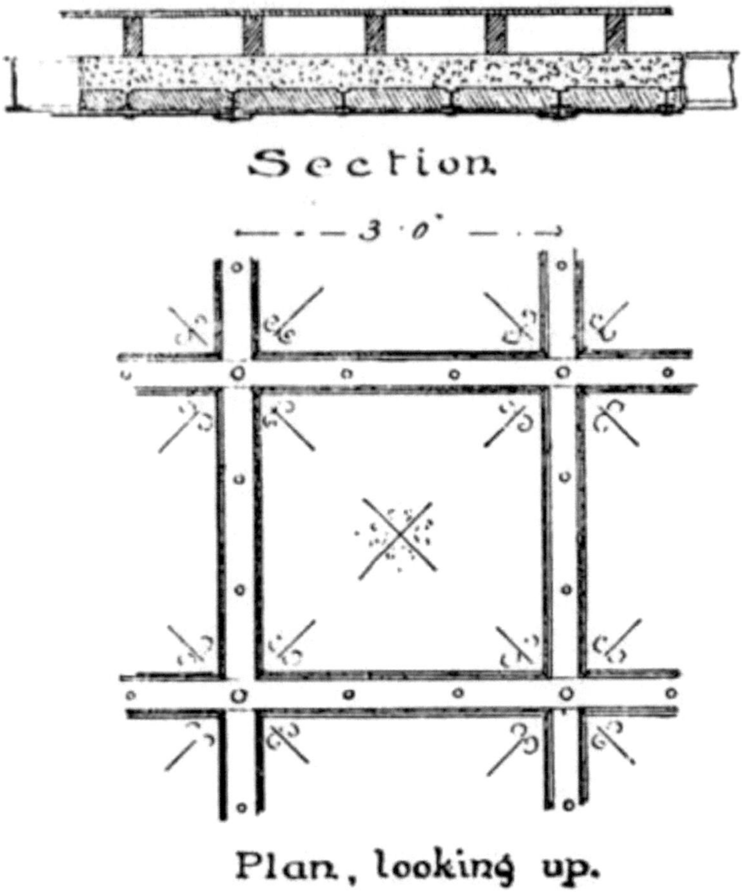

Fig. 18.
Section and Plan of an Enamelled Iron Ceiling.

Glazed brickwork for the walls of hot rooms, &c., should be specified to be executed with an extra neat joint, and should bond to less than 12 in. to the foot; otherwise the effect of the unwieldy mortar joints is clumsy. This applies equally to walling and to arches and vaults. Work which may pass as fair in ordinary cases, looks coarse and rough in the glazed interior walls of a bath. In selecting glazed bricks there is some difficulty in obtaining really delicate tints;

much of the work produced is unfortunately of a very crude colouring. [Pg 108]

One portion of the tepidarium, and other bath rooms, admits of being rendered very attractive; and that is the flooring. Mosaic work is always pleasing, if it be designed with taste and executed artistically. Marble and tile mosaics are both good, the former admitting of a richness of effect quite its own, and the latter of brilliant colouring. In designing marble-mosaic floors, however, one may well fight shy of including that senseless, purposeless description which is nowadays so often employed as a filling-in between borders. I refer to the heterogeneous jumble of every colour mixed without regard to one another, and giving at a distance a dirty grey tone, and near at hand an effect like a gravel walk covered with faded cherry-blossom—to be flattering. Despite the fact that this method of design is of antique origin, and has a real classical designation, I cannot but think that it is to be avoided, and that fillings-in should be made with tesseræ of one tint, or that mosaic should be abandoned altogether.

Given the means, it is easy to render a set of bath rooms elaborate, with faïence and modelled glazed ware, marbles and painted encaustic tiles, and many other suitable but expensive materials; but for my own part I prefer to see comparative simplicity in a sudatory chamber, though by this I do not mean monastic severity of style.

The general air of the frigidarium requires some consideration. It should have an effect of its own, quite distinct from anything else. It should have something of the conservatory in it. It should be richly carpeted, have much woodwork about it, and [Pg 109] be pleasant with plants and laden with the murmur of falling waters. It should be light, certainly; cheerful, cool, and airy looking; and as lofty as possible within reason and common sense. The ceiling should be of a light tone. A lantern-light where the light may come in, rather than be seen, and where the vitiated air may go out, is a pleasant and useful addition.

Points for emphasising with a view to ultimate effect are the stairs to hot rooms—if a staircase be needed—the divans or screens for couches, and an ornamental fountain as above described. The staircase may be rendered attractive with bowl newels, and perhaps white marble treads to the stairs. The divans may be rendered things of beauty by designing ornamental, open-work wood partitions, in either an Oriental style or otherwise. It is not easy to make small dwarf partitions, enclosing a couple of couches, look handsome. As a rule, they are of a flimsy and gimcrack order of architecture. They should be made as solid as possible. For effect there is nothing better than prettily-designed divans.

As regards style, I do not see why one method of design should be more suited than another for the bath. Having become popularly known as the "Turkish" bath, an Eastern or Saracenic style has been often adopted in the past. And, inasmuch as such style is essentially an interior style of architecture, there is something to be said on this score. It is, moreover, a style in which surface decoration pertains rather than modelled work, or, at least, the modelling is in very low relief. There is yet ample scope for the display of skill in the design [Pg 110] of a bath in an Oriental style, as hitherto such attempts have only been made in a half-hearted manner; and in many smaller commercial baths the unskilful use of the style has vulgarised it to no small extent. [3]

Considering that the old Romans brought the bath to a great pitch of excellence—far, very far, I should be inclined to say, in advance of our present knowledge of the subject—their style of architecture would seem fitted to its design at this day; and for large public baths, larger than any yet erected in this country, one can imagine that a very interesting design could be made in the Roman style, founded on a study of the old baths, and, for the sake of the interest attaching to them, reproducing many of the original mosaics, pictures, details, &c., of the public baths of the time of the Empire. In a like manner in the Moorish style one could obtain a very elegant effect by a careful study of old baths in Eastern countries, [4] drawing, perhaps, some inspiration from the courts of the palaces of the Moors, with their pleasant retired air, for the frigidarium. I have often thought, when looking at the late Owen Jones' splendid model at the Crystal Palace, what an admirable frigidarium the Court of the Lions would make, with its [Pg 111] spacious central area, and retired nooks suitable for couches, and its pretty sparkling fountain and green plants, its brilliant colouring, and general cheerfulness of effect. Similarly, in a Roman style, a Pompeian court seems suggestive of the arrangement of a fine frigidarium, with its *cubicula* for couches, and its central area and fountain.

The above are but theoretical suggestions as to what might be done should the bath make such progress in this country as may necessitate the provision of handsome public baths for the people. In everyday practice there is not a great field for elaborate designing in baths. Although only the Roman and Eastern styles have been mentioned, there can be no manner of reason why an architect should not design his bath in whatsoever style he may please.

I have spoken of the plunge bath as a feature capable of being rendered a thing of beauty. This is in reference as much to its plan as to the materials of the sides and floor, &c. There is no reason why a plunge should always be a plain oblong on plan. It may be of any of the shapes indicated at Fig. 19. Many bathers, especially in warm weather, like to stay some minutes in the plunge, and not go straight through; they may like to swim up and down the bath, and thus require room to turn, and a keyhole plan, such as at A, is suitable, and especially useful where the bather has to return to the end of bath he entered. Another shape is shown at B. In ladies' baths still more margin for novel planning is allowable, as here the true dive seldom pertains. A delicate semi-oval plan, such as that at D, [Pg 112] which is much after the pattern of the Roman bath recently discovered at Box, could be employed; or a plain, circular bath with steps around, such as that of the Pompeian *Balneum*, shown at C; or, again, such a plan as that at E, after the classic one at Bognor in Sussex. For inspirations as to the plans of plunge baths, we cannot do better than refer direct to the old Roman remains, either in Italy itself, or in Great Britain and other provinces and colonial dependencies of the old [Pg 113] Empire. The Romans were fully alive to the possibilities of the plunge bath as a subject for artistic design, and often produced baths of great beauty.

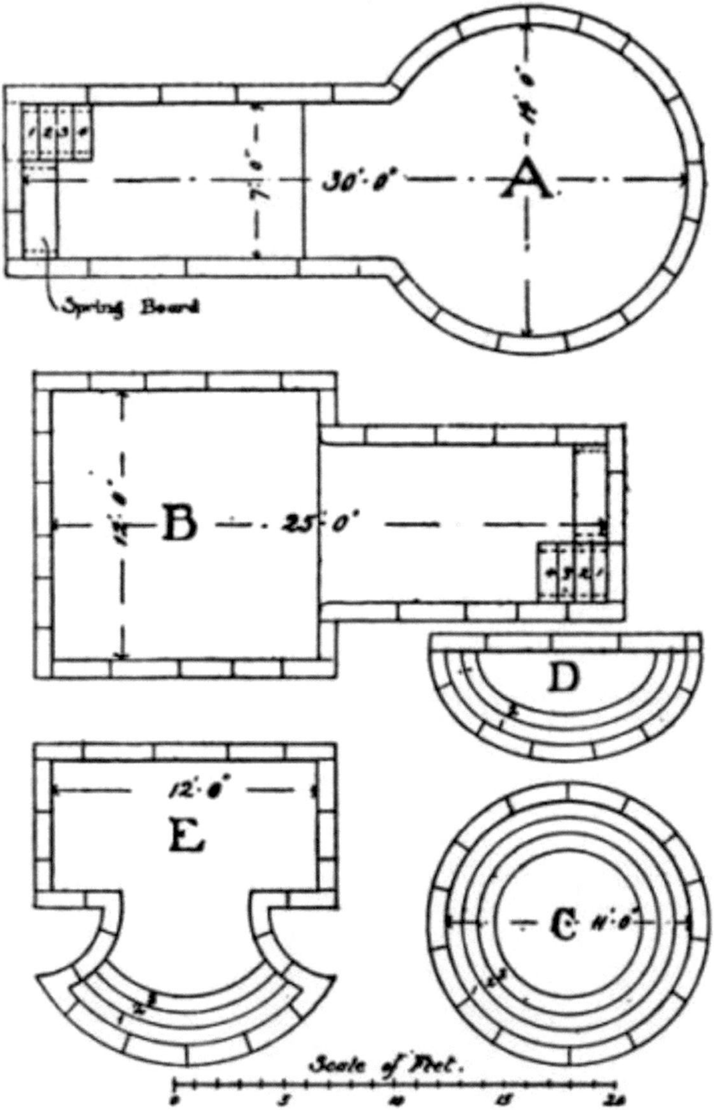

Fig. 19.
Plans of Plunge Baths.

The flooring and sides of these baths should be of a light tint, and there should always be more or less pure white. Nothing really is better than plain white glazed bricks, with neat joints. With this bottom the water always looks clean when it is clean, and shows contamination when it exists. Marble-mosaic floorings should be chiefly of white tesseræ, any simple patterns being executed in light tints. Delicate tints, such as strawberry, pea green, and peacock blue, look well through the water. The floor of the plunge bath may thus be made very pretty. The sides are best of glazed brickwork, neatly executed, and coping and treads of steps of so-called white marble.

Furnishing.

The work of the upholsterer in fitting up a Turkish bath comprises the complete furnishing of the cooling room with couches, lounges, ottomans, carpets, mats, and any chairs and tables that may be required, besides the usual furniture common to all rooms. In the sudatory chambers may be required easy chairs of peculiar construction, with stretched canvas seats; in some cases movable wooden benches in lieu of fixed marble-topped ones; and any carpeting, matting, felt for benches, curtains (if any), and Indian matting for dadoes. These are the principal requirements that need consideration, the remaining furnishing of subordinate [Pg 114] apartments being, of course, of commonplace and ordinary description. The refreshment department requires possibly a coffee-maker, refrigerator, ice-box, and shelf fittings; but, as a general rule, no arrangements for actual cooking.

The cooling room couches are usually made 6 ft. by 2 ft.; but 6 ft. 6 in. by 2 ft. 6 in. is a more liberal allowance. They should be made of polished wood, strongly framed, stuffed with horsehair and covered with a red Turkey twill, as at A, Fig. 21. Where divans are adopted, on the Eastern model, the benches must be framed of wood, permanently fixed, and covered with mattresses kept in their places by a wooden fillet, as Fig. 20. Above the couch thus formed it is well to stretch a dado of Indian matting, affixed above to a moulded rail.

The carpets employed in the cooling room should be soft to the tread. Nothing, of course, equals a Persian or Turkey carpet, and one or the other should be provided when their cost can be afforded. A rich carpet adds greatly to the effect of the room. In cases where a polished wood floor is adopted and shown, soft durable matting or strips of carpet must be placed along any routes, such as from and to the hot rooms and the boot-room, by the sides of couches, to lounges and tables, &c.—anywhere, in fact, where the bather may require to tread. Anything in the nature of fastenings likely, by any possibility, to injure the feet, must be carefully avoided.

A table or two for books, papers, magazines, &c., should be provided in the cooling room. The provision [Pg 115] of lounges, &c., must depend upon the design of the room, and whether nooks or angles are available for their accommodation. Little wooden or metal tripod tables must be placed by the heads of the couches (Fig. 21, B).

[Pg 116]

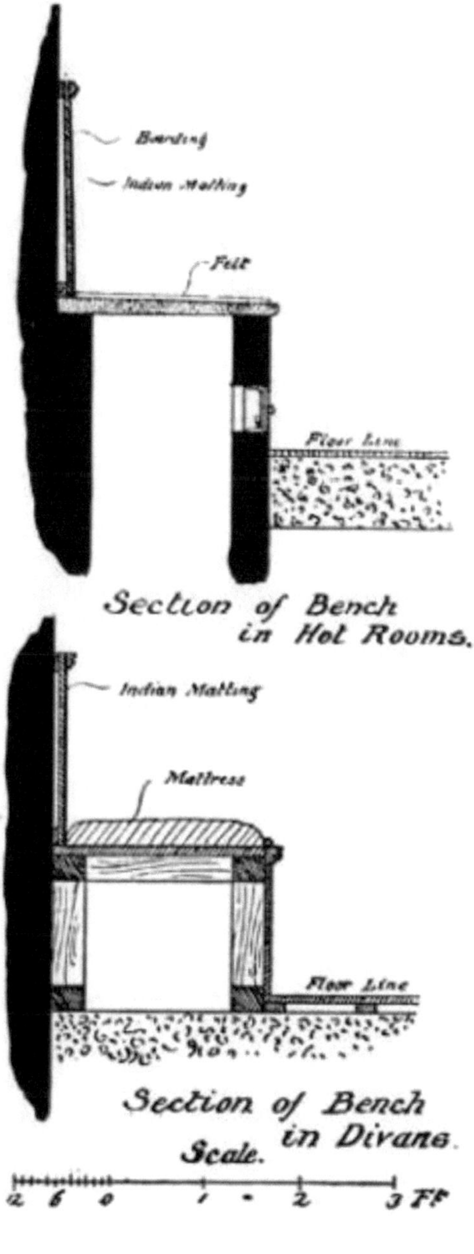
Section of Bench
in Hot Rooms.
Indian Matting
Mattress
Floor Line
Section of Bench
in Divans.
Scale.

Fig. 20.

Section of Benches in Hot Rooms and in Cooling Room Divans.

The chairs in the hot rooms must be designed upon some such lines as at C and D, whereat are shown an iron, and a wooden, framed chair. Beechen frames are best, and the seat formed of rather closely-woven canvas fixed at top and bottom and hanging in a curve. A few of these seats should always be provided in the hot rooms. Movable wooden *benches* are constructed of beech, oak, or well-seasoned yellow deal, as at E. The head end is best raised as shown. Very carefully-seasoned wood should be employed, for all joinery purposes, in the hot rooms.

In the boot room, the pigeon-holes must not be forgotten, and a cushioned seat, perhaps, for taking off boots and shoes. A shelf or shelves for linen checks is useful in this position.

Sometimes the floor of the calidarium is carpeted all over, but *strips* of matting or carpet are better. The hot laconicum is best carpeted throughout. The tepidarium should have strips of carpet where the bathers must necessarily tread. In some baths it is the custom to provide, instead of carpet, felt sandals for use in the hot rooms. For similar reasons to the carpeting—the non-conduction of heat—fine white felting is sometimes placed in strips along the marble benches, as at Fig. 20. Of the Indian matting for a portion of the walls above the benches, I have already spoken. [Pg 117]

In the shampooing rooms, little blocks of wood shaped as at E, Fig. 5, are required as head-rests. They should be about 12 by 5 by 4 in., and hollowed to fit the head.

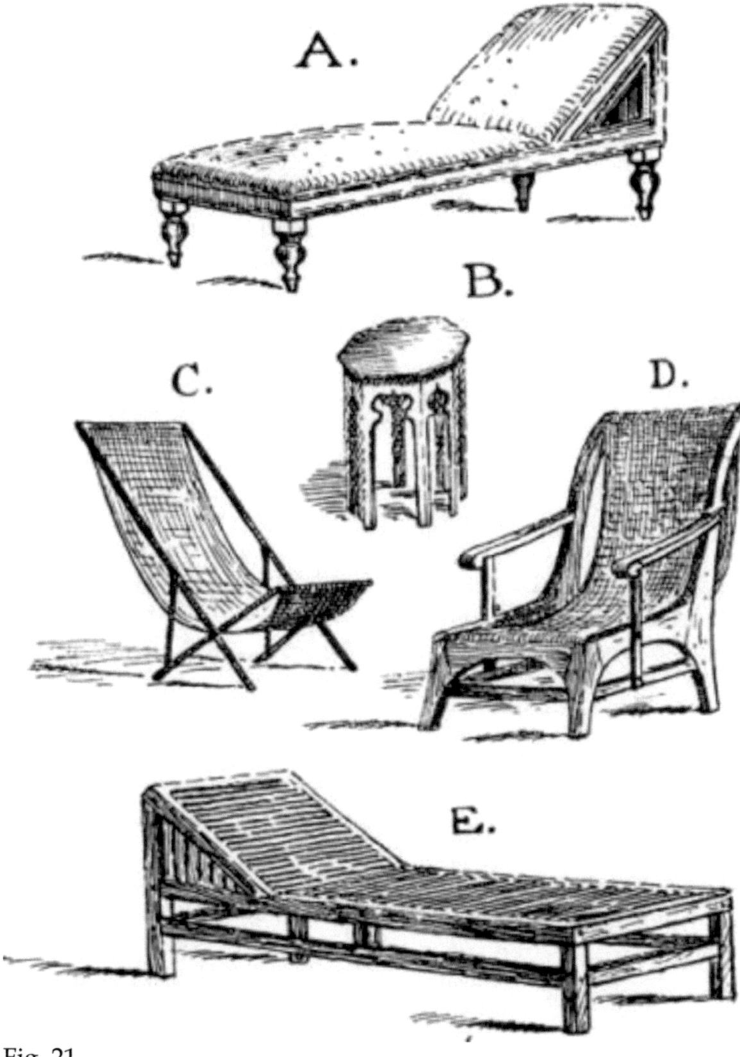

Fig. 21.
Furniture of a Turkish Bath.

[Pg 118]

CHAPTER VIII.

PRIVATE BATHS.

The Turkish bath in the house may be designed on any scale, from a single room heated to the required temperature by a common laundry stove, to an elaborate suite of apartments, providing all that is found in the public bath, and even added luxuries. It may be an addition to an existing building or a feature designed at one and the same time as the house.

There are, of course, many expedients for producing perspiration by heated air much simpler than by the special construction of a suite of bath rooms; but as they will be familiar to all studying the subject of baths, I will pass them over here as mere makeshifts. For although there is something to be said in their favour, in that the head is free and one can breathe cooler air, there are serious objections to their use, as the lamps employed *burn the air*, and there is also an absence of that rapid aërial circulation which is so much to be desired. Besides the actual objections to their use, more or less inconvenience attends the employment of the sheet and lamp (or cabinet and lamp) baths, and there is little of the luxury of a true sudatorium about the extemporised bath, admirable as it may be as a hydropathic expedient. [Pg 119]

The bath in the house may consist of one of the following arrangements:—(1) A single room used as a sudatory chamber and for washing; (2) a hot room and a washing room; (3) a combined hot room and washing room, and a cooling room; (4) a cooling room, washing room, and hot room; or (5) a suite of chambers of such extent as to provide every possible luxury, such as even the old Roman gentlemen would have coveted. Where there is no second room the bather must use his bed room as a cooling and reposing room, as he must also in the cases where only a washing room and a hot room are provided.

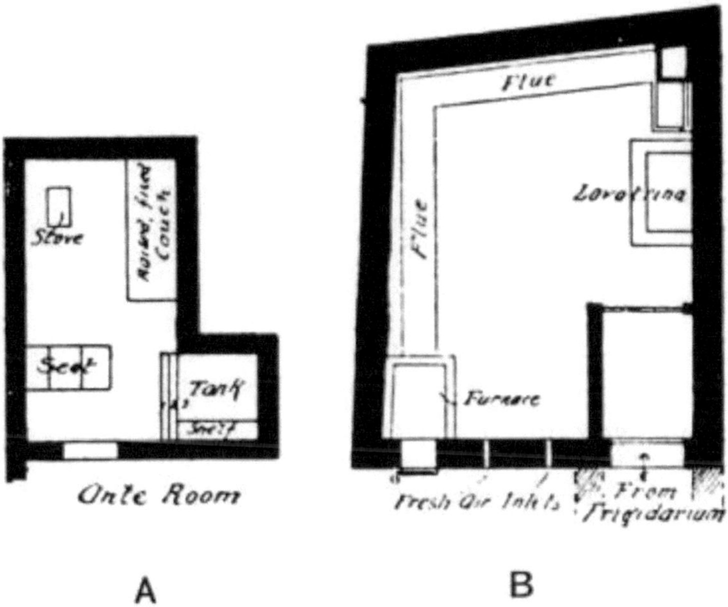

Fig. 22.
Plan of Mr. Urquhart's Small Private Bath and of the Hot Room at Sir Erasmus Wilson's Bath at Richmond Hill.

For a simple sudatory chamber, where washing operations are also conducted, all that is required is a room with brick walls and fire- and heat-proof floor and ceiling, with an adjoining lobby, a flue to conduct smoke from a simple stove, and a sunk washing tank or *lavatrina*. Allowance must be made for a couch [Pg 120] opposite the stove. Fig. 22 (A) shows the simplest form of a bath room possible; it is that which Mr. Urquhart constructed, and has described in his 'Manual of the Turkish Bath.' It was erected by him to show how cheaply an effective bath room might be built, the whole arrangement, with water fittings and building of three of its walls, only costing 37*l*.

The room or rooms forming the Turkish bath in a private house should be cut off by a lobby from the other apartments of the house, with carefully-fitting self-closing doors at either end; and in the case of an elaborate bath, another little lobby with double doors and heavy curtains, should be placed between the cooling room and the two bathing rooms, as at Fig. 24. The air of the hot rooms should, of course, be perfectly and absolutely cut off from that of the house.

The position of the bath in a house will depend upon the size of the bath and the house and its situation. In town houses, where the bath consists of only a washing and a hot room, the first floor will be the most convenient. Where a cooling room is provided, the ground floor is as handy as anywhere; and this position allows of the easier construction of the heating apparatus. In the country, the bath is best built away from the house, connected by a short lobby, which may be utilised for boots, &c., as at Fig. 24. The main difficulties to be overcome are the heating of the bath, and the non-conduction of heat to places where it is not wanted.

The heating apparatus of a private bath may be, for the simplest, a common laundry stove, as at Fig. 22 (A) and at Fig. 23; for bigger baths, a small convoluted [Pg 121] stove, as at Fig. 24; or a furnace of firebrick with an iron flue, as at B, Fig. 22—a plan of the hot room (15 ft. by 12 ft.) of the bath which Sir Erasmus Wilson built at Richmond Hill. For elaborate baths, a small furnace wholly constructed of fireclay, such as that of which I have given complete plans in the chapter on "Heating and Ventilation," would be the best. A furnace of this description is shown in the design for an elaborate private bath, at Fig. 25. Should the bath be heated regularly every day, a firebrick furnace is certainly the best, as such furnaces retain their heat a long time. It should be "banked" at night. A bath only required at times, and quickly, is best heated with a thin iron stove. A portable iron stove and a long length of iron flue will rapidly raise the temperature. The simple baths illustrated at Figs. 22 (A) and 23, are therefore very convenient and effective. The principle of heating by the transmission to the hot rooms of freshly-heated air is also a very convenient one for private purposes, as on this system the bath may be on an upper floor, and yet have its heating apparatus conveniently stowed away below, as at Fig. 24. A small furnace chamber, such as that at Fig. 6, *ante*, must be constructed, and a hot-air flue of large section built up to the hot room. If the bath be on the ground floor, the construction of any form of heating apparatus is rendered easier.

To prevent the transmission of heat to other apartments of the house, the precautions hereinbefore mentioned must be observed. Hollow walls must be provided round the heated chambers, to prevent loss of heat on [Pg 122] the external side, and the transmission of heat through internal walls. The floors above and below should—if not of solid fireproof construction—be formed as described in the section dealing with the design of the sudorific chambers, with puggings of slag-wool, asbestos, sawdust, or materials having similar properties. Windows should be double. Wherever possible, concrete floors should be provided to the hot rooms and washing rooms, so that they may be covered with tiles or mosaics, and on account of the spilling of water. It should be needless to point out the necessity of having most careful regard to safety from fire by the stoves or furnaces.

The ventilation of private baths should receive as much careful attention as those for public use. The hollow external walls may often be used with advantage for the extraction of the vitiated air, which must be let into the cavity at the floor level. If the bath be constructed on the ground floor, with nothing beneath, the system of carrying off the vitiated air by horizontal conduits—recommended for public baths—should be employed, as in the accompanying design for a large private bath, where the whole of the foul air is drawn into one vertical shaft of sufficiently wide section. Much that I have said on the heating and ventilation, and, indeed, on many matters in connection with the design of public baths, applies in the case of the private one, and the reader is therefore referred to preceding pages for many hints as to its construction.

In the accompanying figures I have endeavoured to explain the arrangement and construction of private [Pg 123] baths, from those formed by converting existing rooms into bath rooms, to an elaborate and complete design. Fig. 22 (A) is a plan of Mr. Urquhart's cheap private bath, an apartment only measuring 11 ft. by 16 ft., yet forming an effective sudatory chamber, with simple iron stove, couch, seat, and sunk tank or lavatrina. On this principle I have arranged the plans of the baths adapted to existing rooms in a house, shown at Fig. 23. One plan shows a hot room built on to an existing ordinary bath room. A doorway is formed in the old external wall, and the new chamber constructed with hollow walls, with glazed bricks internally. An extra room would, of course, be thus formed on the floor below. A fireproof floor would be provided, and the pipes from iron stove conducted to old fireplace in bath room, which would become the lavatorium, and undressing room if necessary. A double-doored lobby is formed in the latter apartment, and the slipper bath used as ordinarily. It will be seen that by appropriating the adjoining bed room, a frigidarium is obtained, by taking away the flue-pipe to a new chimney, and knocking a doorway through the old partition wall, thus making a complete set of bath rooms.

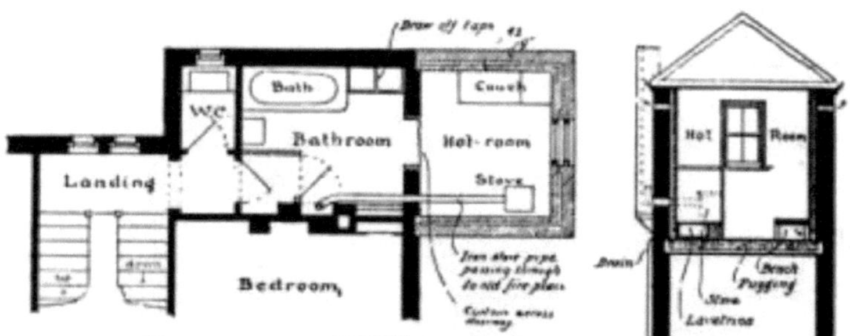

Fig. 23.
Methods of constructing Turkish Baths in existing Houses.
View larger image

The other plan, given at Fig. 23, shows an existing room divided into a combined hot room and washing room, and a cooling room. Three of the walls being ordinary external walls, the hot room is lined with lath and plaster on quartering, leaving an air-space between to prevent loss of heat by absorption and radiation. One or two of the spaces between the quarters should be formed into lath and plaster flues, [Pg 124] for the withdrawal of the vitiated air, being connected below with the hot room, and above lead into the open air. A pugged partition and double-doored lobby separate the rooms. Space is left in the hot room for a full-length couch opposite the radiating stove, which has a metal screen around to protect the more adjacent [Pg 125] walls from the heat. A lavatrina is provided, as shown at the enlarged section. A nook is formed for a shower. This recess could be fitted with enamelled iron screen and hood, as at the end of elaborate slipper-baths. A couple of couches, lavatory, and toilet table are compactly arranged in the little frigidarium.

Where these plain iron radiating stoves are employed, the fresh air should be admitted as near the stove as possible, and if the inlet be connected with a space formed round the stove by a sheet-iron jacket, the air will enter the room at a considerably raised temperature. The temperature of the incoming air in a bath where the heat radiates directly from the stove or furnace to the body of the bather, is not a matter of such vital importance as it is in cases where the heat is transmitted through the agency of the air itself.

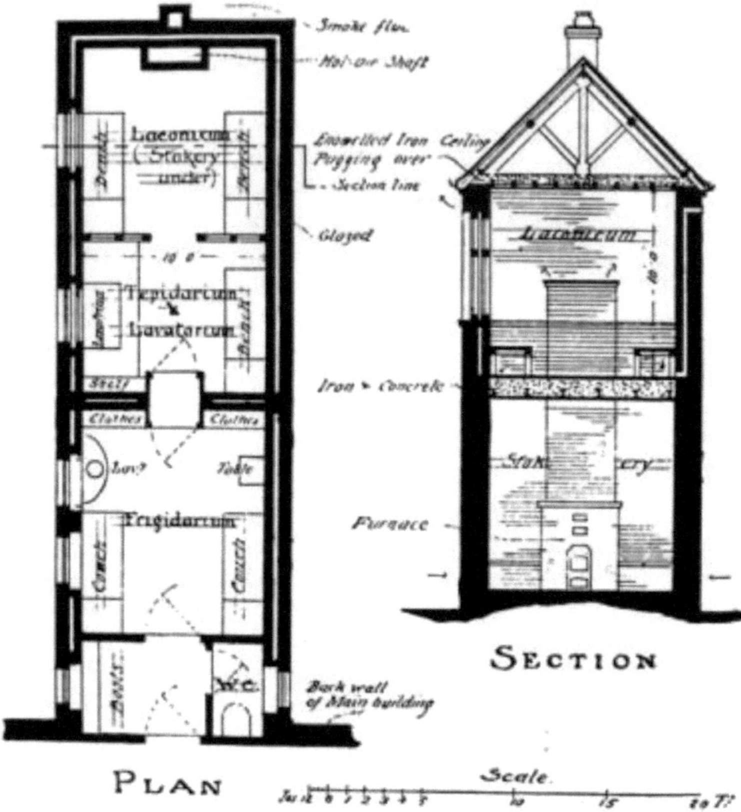

Fig. 24.
A complete Private Turkish Bath.
View larger image

Cost of construction being now so constant a factor in every consideration, I have been led to give the above plans and descriptions of cheaply-formed baths as suggestions for the adaptation of other rooms. But plans of more elaborate baths are occasionally required, and at Fig. 24 I give the plan and cross section of a bath constructed as an appendage to, and at one and the same time as, the house. In this plan all necessaries are liberally provided for, but there is no extravagant outlay on elaboration of features and decoration. It is arranged on the first floor of a projecting wing off the main building. The frigidarium is cut off from the corridor or landing of the house by a lobby, which provides a w.c. and a space for boots and shoes and linen and towels. Between the frigidarium and bath [Pg 126] rooms is a double-doored lobby of a kind that is very useful in both public and private baths. Hung with heavy curtains over the inner face of either door, it forms a perfect preventive against the entry of the air [Pg 127] of the hot rooms into the cooling room. Between the combined tepidarium and lavatorium and the laconicum is a glazed partition with a doorway, fitted with a curtain if necessary. The walls are 18 in.—9 in. and 4½ in., with 4½ in. cavity, used for ventilation. The bath rooms are lined with glazed brickwork. The floor is of fireproof, iron and concrete, construction. Enamelled iron sheets are screwed to the ceiling joists in the hot rooms, and pugging placed over. Under the laconicum is the stokery and furnace chamber, fitted with a small convoluted stove, a hot-air shaft leading to the bath room. Fresh air comes to the stove by horizontal flues from either side of the building. The windows in the bath rooms are double. In the laconicum are two felt-covered wooden benches, as at Fig. 21 (E), *ante*, and a similar bench occupies one side of lavatorium, opposite which is the lavatrina, 18 in. deep, partly sunk into the floor and partly raised. The shower should be placed over this. In the frigidarium are two couches, hooks for clothes, lavatory, and toilet tables, &c. This would be a very effective plan for a comfortable private bath.

The ordinary "slipper," "length," or "shallow" bath is out of place in the rooms of a Turkish bath; but where the bath has to be adapted with economy to an existing bath room, as at Fig. 23, and in cases where, say, some members of a family take the Turkish bath and others the ordinary warm bath, it may remain as at the last-named figure, and serve the purposes of a lavatrina. The lavatrina, as designed in the plan of the large Turkish bath appended, however, is the most convenient apparatus to facilitate the orthodox method of lathering and [Pg 128] washing oneself in this style of bathing, as distinct from the ordinary method of immersion in a large body of water; and as the former manner is the most economical of water, it is unnecessary, in providing a Turkish bath in a house, to make any increased provision for the supply of hot and cold water over and above that which would be allowed for an ordinary slipper-bath.

In a private bath the lavatorium will also serve the purpose of a tepidarium. This chamber should therefore be as large as possible. In it may be required a shampooing slab, and, possibly, a small plunge bath, in addition to the lavatrina, reclining-bench, and what water fittings are to be provided. All that will be required are hot and cold water taps over the edge of the lavatrina, which should also have a waste and overflow. Having to be worked by the bather himself, the shower arrangement should be such as shown at Fig. 17, *ante*. This will serve all purposes, unless a douche and a needle are desired, when the regulating valve of this appliance must be placed conveniently within the bather's reach while standing in the bath.

The private bather, unless he can afford to engage a bath-man, must look upon shampooing as a *luxury* but not a *necessity* of the bath. Dr. W. J. Fleming, in a lecture on the "Physiology of Turkish Baths," read before the Glasgow Physiological Society some years back, said that the accessories of shampooing, &c., are, despite the popular opinion to the contrary, non-essential. A shampooing slab—which must be of marble—is therefore not a necessary provision in any but very elaborate private baths. [Pg 129]

A complete private bath must contain the *piscina*, or plunge. Unless space and expense be no object, this cannot well be made capable of affording a vigorous dive; but endeavours should be made to secure a bath of such dimensions as will admit of a refreshing immersion of the whole body. It will be constructed and fitted exactly as a small public plunge bath.

The frigidarium of a private bath should be as pleasant, cheerful, and comfortable as possible. It should be a cosy place where the bather may recline and cool, and smoke and read, or otherwise divert himself to his heart's content. If so preferred, it might be arranged like an Eastern divan; or it might be a simple, homely room, fitted with one or two comfortable couches. A fireplace may here be a desirable feature, for appearance sake, during the winter months. The room should be *really* ventilated—viz. well supplied with pure, fresh air, and with effective means of withdrawing the vitiated atmosphere, since, as I have pointed out in the chapters on public baths, the cooling process is, in its way, as important as the heating, it being essential that the bather should expose the whole surface of his skin to volumes of pure cool air.

[Pg 130]
[Pg 131]

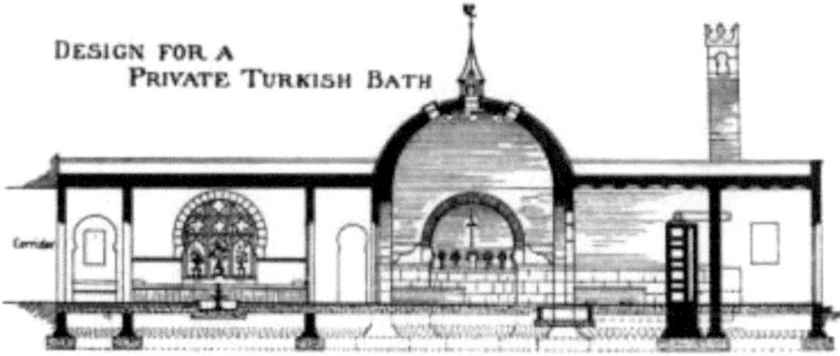

Fig. 25.
Design for a Private Turkish Bath
Longitudinal Section.

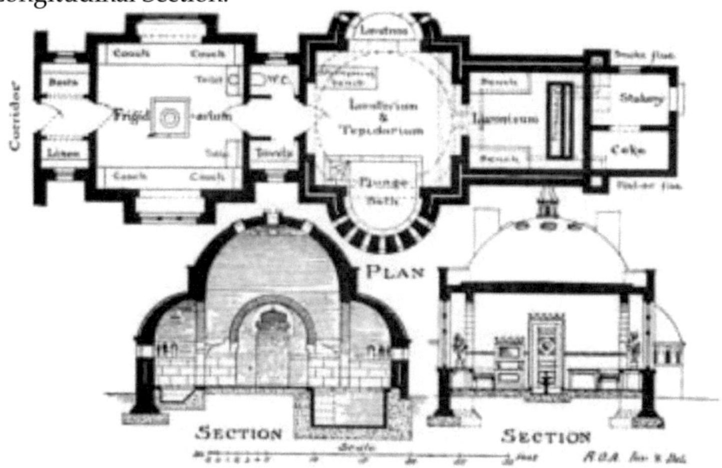

Design for a Private Turkish Bath. View larger image

At Fig. 25, pages 130 and 131, I give plans of a large private Turkish bath. It is such a building as would be a most desirable and pleasing addition to a country mansion; and considering the money prodigally lavished over the appurtenances of the modern mansion house, it is indeed surprising that more has not been attempted in the way of appending a feature that is at once a talisman of health, a cure for disease, and an untold luxury. The [Pg 132] public bath may be a blessing, but for comfort and luxury it cannot compare with the well-appointed private bath.

The design I give as a suggestion, to be modified and adapted to any style of design. The building could be connected to the house by a corridor, or by a glazed *xystos*, either abutting on to the main wall of house or a little detached. Off the lobby to the frigidarium are recesses for boots and for linen. The frigidarium—about 15 ft. square—has benches fitted up like one side of a divan, bay windows with space for plants and flowers, lavatory and toilet-table, and an ornamental fountain. A lobby separates this apartment from the bath rooms, and off it are a w.c. and a towel closet, which latter could be supplied with hot air. The combined lavatorium and tepidarium—14 ft. square—is a domed chamber, with semicircular recesses containing the plunge bath and lavatrina. A shampooing bench is shown. A marble dado surrounds the walls, and marble corbels are provided to pendentives of dome—which could be of brick or terracotta and concrete—and marble springers to horseshoe arches. The shower is placed over the lavatrina. Plenty of space is left for a bench or chair in this chamber. Adjoining is the laconicum with a firebrick furnace, after the nature of that of which I have before given full detailed drawings. The vitiated air is drawn through flues in the floor, to a shaft on the opposite side to the chimney. The stokery and coke-store adjoin the laconicum. Fresh air would be admitted to the furnace as explained in the detailed description of the furnace illustrated at Fig. 10. If there [Pg 133] were no available supply of water from house, a boiler and tank could be placed in the stokery, and a cistern on the flat roof. The flat roof, if of iron and concrete, would form an abutment to dome. If thought desirable, the same flat roof could be carried over the combined tepidarium and lavatorium. An air space should be left between the masonry of dome and covering of copper or other material. The lights should be double glazed. With the radiating stove there is no objection to the loftiness of the dome. This bath could be perfectly ventilated and supplied with pure heat of a most hygienic character. [Pg 134]

CHAPTER IX.

THE BATH IN PUBLIC AND PRIVATE INSTITUTIONS, ETC.

The bath for the hydropathic establishment will generally be required in connection with, and—what is of greater moment—*in harmony with*, other baths, such as medicated baths, Russian or vapour baths, and the ordinary douche, wave, spray, and needle baths, which, where the Turkish bath is included, may often be efficiently administered with the appliances usually provided in the shampooing and washing room. Moreover, if the establishment include the pumilio-pine treatment, or system of pine-therapeutics, there will be required rooms or halls for the inhalation of dry pine and pinal vapour. The nature of the communication between these different baths, as the medicated, Russian, &c., and the Turkish bath, and their relative positions, must be carefully studied. It should be compact and the various passages and corridors as short as possible, these passages and corridors being provided with means for maintaining them at a suitable, and uniformly equable, temperature. This latter point we do not find so carefully studied in hydropathic establishments as its importance would warrant. The consequence is that, in passing backwards and forwards to [Pg 135] and from the different bath rooms, the delicate invalid contracts a serious chill.

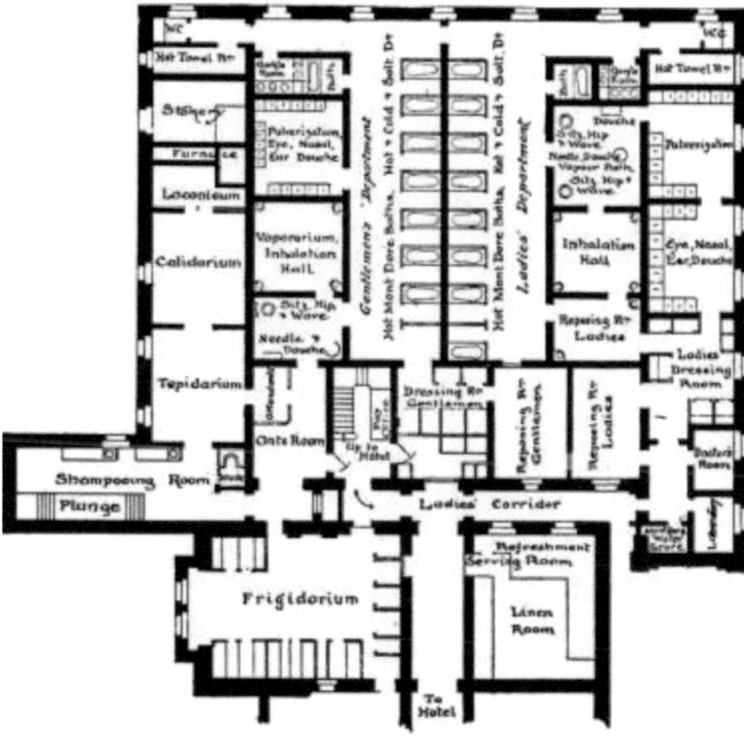

Fig. 26.
Plan of the Baths at the Hôtel Mont Dore, Bournemouth.
View larger image

I give herewith, at Fig. 26, a plan of the baths at the Hôtel Mont Dore, at Bournemouth, which, though not confessedly a hydropathic institution, has yet a fine [Pg 136] bathing establishment of the hydropathic type, as well as complete arrangements for the administration of the pine cure. These baths include a Turkish bath, with three hot rooms, a shampooing room, and cooling room, connected by an anteroom with the suite of miscellaneous bath rooms of the gentlemen's department. The latter comprise a room for the tonic water baths, such as the needle, douche, sitz, hip, and wave; a room or "hall" for the inhalation of pine vapour, whilst in a bath of condensed steam; and a room for the administration of the Mont Dore cure, consisting of the application of pulverised Mont Dore water, or spray, to the eye, nose, or ear, as may be required, this room being also used for the inhalation of dry pine. In addition are a range of slipper baths, in comfortably fitted bath rooms, for the purposes of electric and medicated baths, such as those of pine extract, sulphur, iodine, &c., &c., and for ordinary hot and cold spring-water and salt-water baths. In connection are arranged dressing and reposing rooms, besides necessary subsidiary apartments. A somewhat similar suite of rooms is arranged for ladies on the other side of the block. There is no separate Turkish bath, however; certain days of the week are set apart exclusively for ladies' use. The steam boilers, which supply the steam to the vapour baths and pine-vapour baths, and the water super heaters, as well as the hotel lift and pumping machinery, are arranged in a basement under the stairs, anteroom, tepidarium, and shampooing room.

It will be seen that the compact little Turkish bath, which was arranged under the direction of the late [Pg 137] Mr. Charles Bartholomew, is in direct communication with the other baths, allowing the bather to pass from the hot rooms, or shampooing room, to medicated or pine bath, or *vice versâ*. In designing the plan of baths of the type of those at the Mont Dore, this intercommunication between the various baths is the point to be most carefully studied. Direct communication is required between the Turkish, and the Russian, bath, inhalation hall, and medicated baths, as some methods of treatment render this an absolute necessity.

In a small establishment the hydropathic appliances are movable, and used in ordinary bath rooms, the Turkish bath being the only feature requiring special design.

A true hydropathic establishment of any size should be provided with two Turkish baths, one for ladies and one for gentlemen, as the power and efficiency of the treatment may depend upon the regularity and persistency with which it is carried out. Where there is only one bath, it has to be set apart on different days for the use of ladies and gentlemen, and it is evident that the benefit of a course of baths may be greatly lessened by the occasional unreadiness of the bath. Two suites of rooms should, therefore, be provided. It may be that they will be most economically constructed and worked if arranged side by side, so that they may have their furnaces together, and be stoked with economy.

Where, as in country establishments, there is plenty of room, it is often convenient to arrange the Turkish and other baths on the ground floor adjoining the main building, a corridor of connection being placed, if neces [Pg 138] sary. It should be remembered, however, that invalids have to be taken—often carried or wheeled in movable chairs—to the baths, and allowance should therefore be made for the passage of such a wheeled chair from the top story, by way of a lift, to the door of the baths.

In a large establishment, a full complement of rooms should be provided for the Turkish bath—viz. three hot rooms, a washing and shampooing room, and a cooling room. They will, of course, be on a small scale; but the whole number should be provided. A plunge bath should also be added, but in small hydropathics may be dispensed with altogether.

For hydropathic purposes the lavatorium is generally required to have rather more elaborate water-fittings than other baths. The needle bath should include the ascending shower, the back shower, and the spinal douche—a small nozzle behind the rose of the vertical shower. The regulating appliances for these various showers, sprays, &c., should be brought together, and conveniently placed for the attendant. A very ingenious appliance, suitable for a hydropathic bath, is a thermometer regulating valve, which indicates the temperature of the water being supplied to the bather. The waters mix in a ball, into which is inserted the bulb of a sensitive thermometer, which rises and falls as the hot or cold handles are turned.

If the shampooing and washing room of the Turkish bath is to be used for the administration of the tonic water baths to other bathers besides those taking the Turkish bath, it must be made of ample dimensions. So, also, if the cooling room is to be used as a reposing [Pg 139] room for other bathers, it must be made of large size.

Perfect ventilation is of paramount importance in baths used for the treatment of disease. Purity of atmosphere in the hot rooms is a vital necessity, and so also is it in the miscellaneous bath rooms of a hydropathic establishment.

Unreadiness is a great vice in the Turkish bath appended to these institutions. Hot rooms beneath their proper temperature, and lukewarm water, are unpardonable delinquencies, either in the early morning, in the evening, or during the day. For this reason I would recommend a furnace of fireclay, as it retains its heat for a long time, and is not subject to the rapid changes of iron stoves.

Much of that which I have said with respect to the hydropathic bath will apply to the design of the bath for hospital and asylum purposes. Here, however, efficiency is all that is required, and everything need be but of the plainest description. The conditions and exigencies of each case must determine the size, position, and nature of the suite of bath rooms. All that has been said upon the subject of the design and construction of the bath must be studied, and the principles, herein given, applied to the peculiar circumstances. So also in regard to Turkish baths for hotels, and for residential blocks of buildings, and for clubs.

There is a wide field for activity in Turkish bath building, in the increased provision of baths in hospitals, asylums, and public and private institutions of one kind and another; and also in hotels, "flats," and clubs. [Pg 140] The hydropathic establishments have long adopted the Turkish bath as a powerful remedial and curative agent in perfect harmony with the principles of the Water Cure. But it is only occasionally that such provision has been made in hospitals and asylums; and although within the last few years noticeable innovations have been made in this respect, the subject has heretofore been greatly neglected. Seeing, too, the immense extent to which co-operative living has developed, and the consequent enormous increase in size of large hotels, residential blocks, &c., I cannot but think that the builders of such tenements could with advantage turn their attention to the supplying of small Turkish baths for the visitors and residents. [Pg 141]

CHAPTER X.

THE TURKISH BATH FOR HORSES.

Animals of many kinds, including horses, dogs, cows, sheep, and pigs, have been experimented upon with regard to the bath, and with much success. But for practical purposes all we need here consider is the design of the bath for horses, since a bath for a horse will evidently be suitable for a cow, and might not be wholly beneath the dignity of a pig. It is, after all, only in connection with the training of horses that anything of practical importance has been accomplished in this direction. Several Turkish baths for horses have been erected in this country in connection with hospitals for horses, attached to large businesses, and appended to training stables. In the development of race-horses the treatment has, according to the opinion of several authorities, been found eminently beneficial.

The bath must be arranged in connection, and in direct communication with the stables. It may consist, as Fig. 27—a plan of a bath built for the Great Northern Railway Company's hospital for horses—of a washing, and two hot, rooms. An airy shed will do for a place for the animals to cool, and in fine weather they will derive more benefit from being turned out in the open. In the plan given it will be seen that the horse is led [Pg 142] through the washing room into the first hot room. Without turning round, he may be led into the second hot room and thence into the washing room again. In the hot rooms, which are heated by a convoluted stove, are stocks, wherein, if restive, the animal can be secured. A similar arrangement is made in the washing room, where, after undergoing the sweating process, the horse is groomed down, an operation that should be performed in part with an iron *strigil*, much after the pattern of those employed upon their own bodies by the ancient Romans.

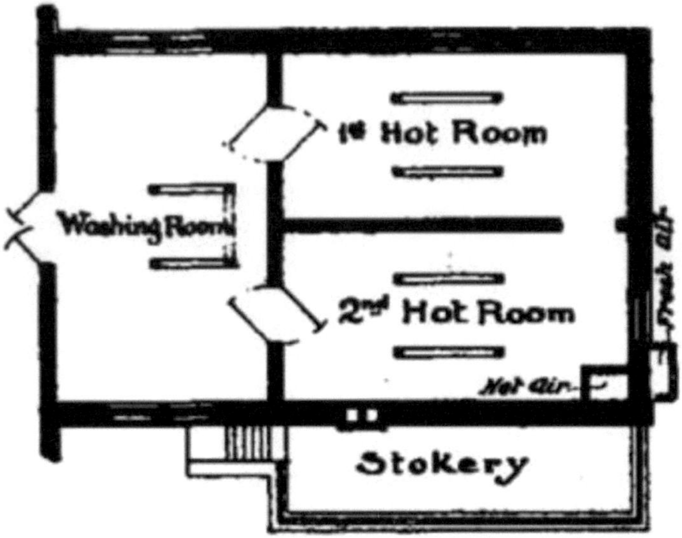

Fig. 27.
Plan of the Great Northern Railway Company's Turkish Bath for Horses.

These equine Turkish baths need be very inexpensive and simply constructed, though, where it is desired to do the thing well, glazed bricks should, for the sake of cleanliness, be used for lining the walls. All that will be required in the washing rooms is a couple of draw-off taps with hot and cold water, some pails, a [Pg 143] scraper, and wash-leather. On leaving the sudatory chamber, the horse should first be well scraped with the scraper, carefully sponging, or dousing him, if necessary, with warm water. Buckets of hot, tepid, and cold water should then be thrown over him, and having been well rubbed down with the leather, he should then be covered with a cotton sheet, and his legs bandaged with cotton bands, the sheets, &c., being gradually removed after an interval of about a quarter of an hour, and the animal turned into a shed, or into the open, to cool.

THE END. [Pg 144]

FOOTNOTES

[1] The Germans, with more perception and accuracy than ourselves, term the therapeutic agent that we called the Turkish bath, the "Roman-Irish bath"—the *Römisch-irische Bäder*. Both the ancient Roman bath and the old Irish "sweating-house," gave out radiant heat from the walls to the bather, and did not depend on the supplying of hot air.

[2] Not *draughts*. The ancient Romans, it is curious to note, would walk in the open air after the bath; and both the *Frigidarium* of the Romans and the *Mustaby* of the Turks were, and are, open to the heavens.

[3] I do not know of any building—bath or otherwise, civil or domestic—in this country where the true spirit of Oriental colour decoration has been grasped. One of the chief principles which seems to have been missed is that in real Saracenic art the colours are employed in very small portions only, and no colour becomes insubordinate to the general effect.

[4] Here is a branch of architectural design absolutely unstudied. Few architects visit the East, and none enter the baths there, either in Egypt, Turkey, or Morocco. The ordeal of the true Oriental shampooing doubtless deters the few who might be curious about these buildings.